TIMBER

A HISTORY OF THE
TIMBER TRADE FEDERATION

TIMBER

A HISTORY OF THE TIMBER TRADE FEDERATION

Robert Fitzgerald & Janet Grenier

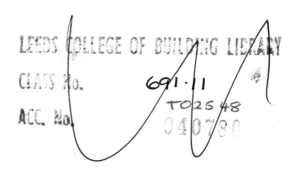
B.T. BATSFORD LTD · LONDON

First published 1992

© Timber Trade Federation 1992

Typeset by Servis Filmsetting Ltd, Manchester

and printed in Great Britain by Butler and Tanner, Frome, Somerset

Published by

B.T. Batsford Ltd
4 Fitzhardinge Street
London W1H 0AH

A catalogue record for this book is available from the British Library

ISBN 0 7134 7101 8

Jacket illustration:

Barge and yard, Maple Wharf, Bow, London, 1930s.

Courtesy of C. Blumson Ltd, Barking, Essex.

—CONTENTS—

— PREFACE —

To mark its centenary in 1992, the Timber Trade Federation of the United Kingdom decided to commission a book which would record the history and the role of timber in the British economy. It immediately occurred to us how little had been written about this very important commodity, yet the supply of overseas timber underpinned a number of industries, especially that of building, and not only was wood one of Britain's principal imports but Britain has been a central market of its international trade. Until the Second World War, it was the world's largest importer of the commodity. By tracing the development of the TTF and its members, we hope that this book will make some contribution to trade and business history, two subjects not too frequently joined. Moreover, it is easy to ignore sectors of the economy because, their firms being of a comparatively small size, evidence is often difficult or impossible to acquire.

There is, as usual, a long list of people whose help should be given public recognition. At the TTF, the Director General, Austin Lockyer, instigated the whole project, provided much of the background material, and oversaw the completion of the book. Michael James, the Public Relations Executive and Director of the Forests Forever Campaign, acted as our liaison, and dutifully read and advised us on our manuscript. Leo Groth, the President, was also actively involved with the project, and, in carefully scanning our text, proved a plentiful source of help and information. He corrected numerous technical errors. Many past officers of the Timber Trade Federation and the Timber Research and Development Association agreed to be interviewed: G.N. Donaldson, R.E. Groves CBE, E.M.L. Latham, T.S. Mallinson, P.B. Meyer, J.G. Sunley, L.A. Woodburn-Bamberger, and J.G. Wright. Mr Donaldson, moreover, provided personal papers and photographs, and Mr Mallinson's comments on Chapter V were detailed and highly informative. Many of the staff at Clareville House, the TTF's headquarters, and especially the Office Manager, Miss Jean Rennie, also deserve thanks.

There are a number of academic credits, too. Fiona Wood at the Business History Unit, LSE did much of the initial, painstaking statistical work. Terry Gourvish, the

Director of the Business History Unit, looked at the manuscript. Charles Feinstein, All Soul's College, Oxford, confirmed suspicions of the pitfalls awaiting anyone who developed an interest in timber statistics, and Jorma Ahvenainen, University of Jyvaskyla, forwarded his very useful articles on the Finnish timber industry. Lastly, the Forestry Commission, the Business Archives Council, the Canadian Embassy in London, *The Timber Trades Journal*, the Council of Forest Industries (BC, Canada), the Province of British Columbia Ministry of Forests, the Swedish-Finnish Timber Council, the World Wide Fund for Nature, and the Friends of the Earth all helped in some form.

Any assistance, moreover, was generously given and no-one attempted to impose any particular line upon us. Consequently, the views expressed in this book are, without exception, entirely our own. We do not expect everyone will agree at all points with our emphasis and interpretation, but we hope for some measure of acceptance amongst the separate worlds of the timber business, academia and the interested public.

ROBERT FITZGERALD

Centre for Management Studies
Royal Holloway and Bedford New College
University of London

JANET GRENIER

Business History Unit
London School of Economics
University of London

—INTRODUCTION—

Understandably, as the Timber Trade Federation celebrates its Centenary in 1992 the Board of Management and the Honorary Officers took the view that the occasion should be marked by the publication of a book dealing with the Federation's history during those one hundred years.

As a trade we only had one 'history book' – Bryan Latham's *The History of the Timber Trade Federation of the United Kingdom: the first Seventy Years*, which was published in 1965 and, given the changes that have taken place in our trade since then, there was an obvious need for a work to bring us right up to date with both our past and recent developments.

This book provides not only a chronological account of our history as a trade but gives at the same time an analytical account dealing with the underlying factors which created the need for a timber trade and its role in Britain's economic history.

The book also takes account of how our trade has structured, and indeed restructured itself to deal with changing economic climates and logistical innovations. There is not a great deal of 'what happened when' or 'who did what and when'. In other words it provides an economic historian's approach to the subject and should provide very interesting reading, especially for those who joined our trade in the last few years, unlike those of my own generation who think they know our history already. I can only say to my contemporaries that there is a great deal in this work which will be of great interest to us as well.

LEO GROTH

President, TTF

L.C.L. Groth, President of the TTF.

I

TRADE AND ORGANISATION

I: A BASIC RESOURCE

Timber ranks as one of the most vital of raw materials, yet logging and silviculture have been unduly overlooked as economic activities. Indeed, the increasing use of timber has been a significant element of world economic history, and, during the latter half of the 19th century, it indicated an improving trend in living standards. Due to differences in the sources of supply and demand for the raw material, timber also constituted a major part of international trading relationships, and it was Britain – a country of growing real wages, high *per capita* consumption, and depleted forests – which became the world's largest importer. The country's purchases were critical to the development of the softwood trade from Europe and, in particular, from the pine and spruce forests around the Baltic; it drew additionally upon the hardwoods of temperate North America and on those found in the tropics.

Timber's chief function has been the provision of shelter, and wood has been employed in the structure of buildings and for the purposes of interior design. In Britain, as elsewhere, the timber trade has been intrinsic to the construction industry, and, as a consequence, it has been influenced by building cycles. Likewise, the availability and price of timber have helped determine building activity and costs, and the development of the timber trade and its organisation have been central to this process.

Wood had other important industrial linkages, too. It not only supported indigenous sawmilling, but was the furniture industry's main material. Timber was required, moreover, for the making of barrels and boxes: coopers needed to import staves; improvements in plywood created the tea-chest and similar receptacles; and the pulp, paper and packaging industry was, of course, similarly dependent upon forest products. Furthermore, timber contributed to the fullest exploitation of energy resources, not because of firewood but because coalmines were held up with timber pitprops. By providing the wherewithal for railway sleepers and telegraph poles, wood was also used in communication services, and conveyance of the material all over the

Vessel carrying first cargo of Douglas Firm (Oregon Pine) to Hull, 1909.
Courtesy of Meyer International, London.

world supported various shipping and internal transport networks. Lastly, minor industries needed wood for the production of numerous articles like toys, brooms and tools. Although the uses of timber have declined in the 20th century, fairly obviously in the case of barrels and pitprops, the raw material has remained central to packaging and furniture despite the arrival of substitutes such as plastic, and the building industry has continued to employ wood despite advances in concrete technology. Timber has maintained its trading importance to Britain, because the high level of need cannot be met through indigenous resources.

The existence of this heavy demand in Britain – for a wide variety of end-uses – stimulated worldwide production and transactions in timber, and established a significant trading and consumer interest at home. As a consequence, some assessment of the role, purpose, and operations of this trade will help us appreciate its impact upon the British economy. It will, in addition, provide the background for analysing the structure of the trade and the effectiveness of its responses to changes in the level and nature of demand. On this point, the history of this business' representative organisation, the Timber Trade Federation, will be illustrative. Its early years, for example, were devoted to the resolution of an issue central to the success of its members. Dealing in a bulky, internationally-traded commodity, timber firms were directly affected by matters of transport, and, as in the 1890s these became a problem with political as well as commercial dimensions, they needed a representative organisation (*see* Chapter II). Because timber was a varied product cut in a plethora of forms and sizes, and because it was obtained from all over the world and transported on a global scale, the trading network was a complicated one composed of many small firms differentiated by function and stages in the production process. The TTF naturally reflected this system, and in the inter-war period became the medium through which restrictive practices sought to maintain traditional arrangements against falling prices and intense competition (*see* Chapter III). For some 30 years after the Second World War, the Federation was embroiled in issues of restrictive practices and industrial restructuring as well as a host of minor issues (*see* Chapter IV). Finally, the TTF has assumed a key role in the marketing of timber (*see* Chapter V). Its existence enables the historian to look at the type of trade where the smallness of firms and lack of records often prohibit investigation, despite the economic significance of its activities.

What, then, was the role of trade in the British economy during the latter half of the 19th century, and how significant was the trade in timber? It is no coincidence that industrial growth has coincided with the internationalisation of trade. The export and import of manufactured goods and commodities allowed countries to make productivity gains, since they enabled specialisation in economic activities best suited to natural and human factor endowments in return for products more efficiently made abroad. Specialisation in many cases also brought returns to scale, and countries with particular strengths could maximise their advantages by selling to overseas markets. The optimisation of comparative costs and prices eventually locked countries into a pattern of trading connections, although sometimes, of course, governments would seek to encourage less efficient, indigenous production by penalising imports.

The uneven distribution of resources also encouraged trade: it was, for one, unlikely that the geographical availability of timber types in the right quantity would perfectly suit the place of its demand. The development of world trade in the 19th century was aided by improvements in internal transport brought by the railways and in external connections as a consequence of expanding shipping fleets, steam power, falling freight rates, and harbour construction. By 1913, the world volume of foreign trade per capita appears to have risen to over 25 times the level of 1800, whereas world output per head had grown by a ratio of 2.2. Therefore, as world trade equalled some 33 per cent of output in the year before the Great War, the figure may have been some 3 per cent in 1800. Trade had become proportionately more important.

Economic specialisation explains the greater and increasing importance of international commerce, but so did the entry of some countries into the world network. Although some developing countries with initially high foreign trade contributions such as the United States and Australia came to rely more upon internal developments, the lack of resources compared to population size in industrialised Europe and Japan, and the availability of primary products in less developed parts provided a basis for trade's relatively fast growth. Europe, including Russia, was responsible for nearly 70 per cent of world trade in 1876–80 and for 62 per cent in 1913. Moreover, the volume of the export trade in primary products like timber more than trebled, the bulk of it destined for Europe. The United Kingdom alone absorbed nearly 30 per cent of world imports in 1876–80 and, despite industrialisation and growth overseas, it still drew 19 per cent of the total in 1913. To pay for these goods, it respectively forwarded some 38 and 25 per cent of world exports. These figures, furthermore, do not emphasise Britain's growing dependence on the importation of basic necessities. By 1900, the value of all imported goods amounted to over 27 per cent of Gross Domestic Product; the figure was nearly 31 in 1910, 34 in 1920 and still 24 in 1930, when the comparable ratio for the United States was 5.0. This amounted to a strategical vulnerability fully exploited by the country's enemies in the course of two world wars. During the post-1945 period, Britain's import dependency ranged between 20 and 25 per cent, and it was significantly above major competitors such as the US, France, Germany, Italy and Japan until the 1970s.[1]

Britain's ability to import food and raw materials, and the falling price of these goods in the last three decades of the 19th century was linked to its specialisation in the production of manufactured goods and to a general rise in living standards. This increase in output and the greater expansion of trade can be easily demonstrated (*see* Table I).

Opposite page: Auction. 'For Sale by Candle', Garraway's Coffee House, 1845.
Courtesy of James Latham Plc, Clapton, London.

FOR

SALE by the CANDLE

AT

Garraway's Coffee House,

'Change Alley, Cornhill,

On THURSDAY, 15th DECEMBER, 1842,

At Half-past Six o'Clock precisely,

By Order of the Importers,

THE FOLLOWING GOODS:—

---

459 Logs Honduras Mahogany, of superior quality, and good dimensions, being the entire cargo of the
GEORGE CANNING,
just landed at the East Wood Wharf, West India Docks.

CONDITIONS OF SALE.

I. THE highest bidder in time to be the buyer, and if any dispute arise, the lot to be put up again and re-sold.

II. The buyers to pay a deposit of *Twenty per Cent.* for each lot, (if required,) and One Shilling per lot to the broker.

III. The goods to be cleared and taken away, with all faults, at the buyer's expense, within fourteen days from the Sale, and to be paid for on or before the delivery.

LASTLY. Upon failure of complying with these Conditions, the deposit to be forfeited, the lots re-sold, either by public or private Sale, and the deficiency (if any) together with all charges, to be made good by the defaulter at this Sale.

Approved Bills at Four Months admitted in payment, or $2\frac{1}{2}$ per Cent. Discount allowed for Cash.

TABLE I

GDP at factor cost, GDP at factor cost per head, exports values, and import values in constant terms, 1870 and 1913 – United Kingdom

	1870	1913	% increase
	(£m & 1913 = 100)		
GDP at factor cost	1012	2133	210
GDP per head at factor cost	32	47	147
Export values	271	710	270
Import values	353	896	254

Source: B.R. Mitchell, *British Historical Statistics*, 1990.[2]

Moreover, the rate of industrialisation, economic expansion and population growth outstripped the domestic supply of food, raw materials, and commodities. As we have noted, Britain overcame this problem of limited natural factor endowments by paying for required imports through industrial specialisation, trade and exports. The benefits in terms of economic welfare are notoriously difficult to gauge, but for the average urban worker real wages increased by some 60 per cent between 1860 and 1900. It should be acknowledged, however, that the rise was uneven and largely attributable to the fall in commodity prices in 1875–96 and to the economic boom of 1897–99, and that living standards were stagnant – and perhaps declined – between the depression of 1900 and 1913. Another sign of improved well-being in Britain during the latter half of the 19th century was the growth in consumers' expenditure from £858m in 1860 to £2,194m in 1913 (1885 = 100).[3]

The consumption of timber also serves – like many a basic material and commodity – as an indicator of well-being, and it was imported into Britain in ever larger proportions. Indeed, imports can be treated as an accurate measure of the British timber trade's fortunes, because indigenous forests had long since ceased to provide the country's needs. A substantial colonial trade had existed in specialist timber since the 17th century, when mahogany, for one, was exported from the Spanish colonies via Jamaica, much of it to be used by furniture makers like Chippendale and Hepplethwaite. By the end of the 18th century, however, Britain's forests could no longer supply even its basic, everyday requirements. Due to the wars in North America, the country had to depend upon European, mostly Norwegian softwoods, only some 1 per cent of timber coming from the colonies. In 1800, therefore, the value of timber arriving in Great Britain reached £543,000 or some 0.8 per cent of total imports.

When Napoleon introduced his Continental System, thus enforcing a European-wide blockade, Britain, once more, became reliant on Canada. Differential tariffs, disadvantaging the Baltics and favouring the colonies, were introduced to lessen

Britain's strategical vulnerability. Until 1821, colonial timber entered free, but even after that date it gained from tariffs granting a 5:1 preference. By 1830, only 24 per cent of timber imports were of non-colonial origin. Wood, nonetheless, later became a focus of free trade agitation, the commercial benefits of purchasing from the nearby and plentiful softwood forests around the Baltic being apparent. Changes in the levels of duty in 1860 effectively ended preference, and the tariff was formally repealed in 1866.[4] The growth in the British timber trade and import levels can be discerned (*see* below).

TABLE II

Timber and Wood imports into the UK. Wholesale prices in £m at current and constant values

Date	Current Value	Price index (1890 = 100)	Constant Value	% of Total Imports Constant Values
1860	6.9			3.3
1866	12.3			4.4
1870	13.1			4.3
1880	16.7	127.0	13.1	4.1
1890	16.7	100.0	16.7	4.0
1895	16.4	83.5	19.6	3.9
1900	27.9	94.5	29.5	5.3
1910	26.2	79.8	32.8	3.9
1913	33.8	90.3	37.4	4.4
1921	30.0	198.6	15.1	2.8

See: Appendix II.

Not only did the real value of the timber trade increase in the 19th century, but until the First World War it continued to account for a substantial and growing proportion of the total import bill. Between 1870 and 1890, the value of timber imports nearly doubled, and then doubled again between 1890 and 1913, despite economic depression during the Edwardian years. The importance of this trade can also be demonstrated: by 1913, timber was still Britain's fifth largest import; it accounted for 4.4 per cent of the total; and was overshadowed only by grain and flour amounting to 10.5 per cent, while raw cotton was at 9.9, meat and animals at 7.4, and raw wool at 4.6. The fall in the percentage attributable to timber after 1900 stems from the increasing consumption of imported consumables like meat, butter and margarine. The absolute and relative decline during 1914 and 1921 – the years of the war economy – was a short-lived phenomenon caused by enforced supply shortages, controls on consumer demand, and rampant inflation.

In addition to the expanding value of the timber trade, volumes and consumption per head showed a significant upward trend (*see* Table III).

TABLE III

Timber Imported into UK, 1851–1913

Year	Total Imports (millions m³)	Per Cap Imports (m³)
1851	2.6	0.09
1861	3.9	0.13
1871	5.9	0.19
1881	8.3	0.24
1891	9.4	0.25
1901	13.4	0.32
1911	13.7	0.30
1913	16.4	0.38

Source: Appendices III & V.

These figures, moreover, do not account for imports of manufactured items containing wood such as toys, games, brooms, brushes, and furniture, and, by 1913, the average UK resident was probably consuming between 0.45 and 0.48 cubic metres of wood. Consumption was not even, of course, and 0.14 cubic metres is a more accurate estimate for Ireland. The existence of indigenous sources of wood should be noted, although the contribution was small. Average annual imports of 16.1m cubic metres in 1909–13 dwarfed a domestic cut of 1.3m, but, with exports and re-exports amounting to a miniscule 0.2m, Britain was, before the Great War, consuming 17.2m cubic feet of wood per year. The bulk of this trade was in sawn softwood timber – in the form of planks, flooring, strips, plaster lath, moulding, and weather boards – and was used by the construction industry. But pitwood imports remained significant, accounting for about a quarter of the total by weight between 1900–13 (*see* below).

TABLE IV

Categories of Timber Imports into the UK by Weight and Value. Annual Average for 1900–13

Category	%Weight	% Value
Sawn Timber	61.4	64.4
Pitwood	25.7	11.2
Hewn & Round Timber	7.9	10.7
Tropical Timber	3.6	11.1
Staves	1.4	2.6

Source: Board of Trade Returns.

Stockholm 9th June 1881

Sold to Messr Horsley, Smith & Co., Hull.

Bought of **The STORA KOPPARBERGS BERGSLAG of STOCKHOLM**

a Parcel of about *921 Standards* Wood Goods to be shipped at **Gefle** and to consist of about the specification below.

The Goods to be of usual quality, according to their respective descriptions at the Port of Loading, and to be ready for shipment *15th August nest*

	SELDOM DRY WAY					Price			
	third 3rd	*4th*	*5th months*			*Redwood*	*White*		
							third 3rd 4th 5th months		
4 x 11	—	—	20	20	20	£ 11. 9: 6.10 5.10	6:-		
3 x 11	15	40	15	50	—	— — 5.10 4.10	5.		
3 x 9	15	40	15		7.	— — 5:- 4:-	—		
3 x 7	—	—	100	110	6				
2½ x 7	—	—	60	120					
2 x 7	—	—		36					
1 x 7	—	—	20	21	—				
1 x 6	—	—		18					
	30	80	486	109	206				

Ends 6 to 8 feet for stowage included in the above quantities, at ²⁄₃ᵈˢ prices of longer lengths.

The prices are in British Sterling per St. Petersburg St:d H:d, all free alongside the ship at **Gefle**.

The goods are warranted to be of fair average quality of the sellers' usual shipment from port of loading and to be delivered free alongside the ship according to the custom of the port, but the sellers are not to be responsible for any deterioration of quality occasioned by circumstances beyond their control after the goods having been sent alongside the vessel.

The buyers undertake in due time either to send out ships to load these goods, giving a sufficient number of working days for loading, or to give the sellers authority to charter for the buyers' account on best possible terms, but without any responsibility whatever.

Payment for the above goods by approved acceptances of sellers' drafts, payable in London at four months from date of Bill of Lading, and if any freight advance be given, the same to be paid by buyers' acceptance at one month from date of Bill of Lading, all on receipt of and in exchange for the shipping documents.

Should any portion of said goods not be removed before the *1st November nest* the buyers to accept as above for the approximate amount of the goods at four months from the said date, the goods lying at the expense of the sellers, but for account and risk of the buyers. Fire insurance to be covered by *the Buyers*

Should the sellers by reason of War, Restraints of Rulers, Fire, Flood, Drought or other accident beyond their control be unable to deliver the whole or any portion of the goods, sellers to have the option of cancelling this contract to the extent of such damage, provided timely notice be given thereof to buyers, sellers however adopting any charter previously closed.

STORA KOPPARBERGS BERGSLAGS STYRELSE

J. E. Kihlman

Horsley Smith & Co.
H.

Stora Kopparbergs Berslag of Stockholm, Bill of Sale to Horsley, Smith & Co., Hull, 1881.
Courtesy of Meyer International, London.

The modern timber trade was established in the latter half of the 19th century, because the easing of import restrictions and the rise in levels of demand opened up new areas of supply and established shipping and commercial networks. As we have seen, the earlier decades of the 19th century saw the provenance of British timber imports shifting from Europe to Canada and the colonies. A change in mercantilist policy had an immediate impact on the country's predominant supplier, Norway, and, to a lesser extent, Finland. But, to meet growing and unprecedented levels of demand towards the middle of the century, supplies had once more to be found and brought from the Baltic. While Canada was responsible for over half of Britain's timber imports in 1850, the figure was below a fifth twenty-five years later. The figures do not demonstrate a secular decline in the Atlantic trade but the rapid rise of North European forest shipments, and the lifting of preferential tariffs between 1860 and 1866 merely marked and spurred the development of British demand for softwoods.

At first, Norway resumed its place as Britain's most important European supplier, because of its long-standing advantage: its forests were located near to ports best positioned for export to Western Europe. Soon, however, the strength of rising demand opened up the economic potential of the Swedish forests, despite initial problems. The bulk of Sweden's sawmilling operations were at this time conducted by peasant farmers undertaking a seasonal occupation in direct response to cash advances from coastal merchants. From the 1860s onwards, exporters and merchants – possessing finance and commercial connections – began to found sawmills near to ports and navigable rivers, particularly at the west coast port of Gothenburg. Later, Stockholm and other ports were developed, so facilitating the exploitation of areas like Norrland. Investment also spread the use of steam-power and increased the size of sawmilling operations. It was both a production and marketing necessity: it enabled demand to be met, brought returns to scale, and satisfied British customers who required sawn goods such as boards, deals and battens.

Exporters were assisted in 1863 by the repeal of mercantilist legislation once designed to protect Sweden's indigenous forest, limit output and maintain prices. Between 1850 and 1872, the volume of Swedish timber exports quintupled. Fifteen per cent of the country's export values in 1846–50, its wood trade accounted for a figure of 51 per cent in 1866–70, and, consequently, became by a large margin Sweden's most important export. Moreover, some £1.5m of its £3.5m annual timber exports were forwarded to Britain. By 1873, the country had replaced Canada as Britain's principal importer: since 1850, its exports had grown from 10 to some 25 per cent of all timber arriving in Britain. In sum, Sweden had by the 1870s overcome its one-time backwardness in sawmilling and transport, and overcome natural disadvantages that stemmed from its dearth of western seaboard and more inaccessible forests. By then an established industry, its timber operations were no longer plagued by financing and liquidity difficulties. So, Sweden maintained its market share in Britain throughout the rest of the century, when volumes continued to grow despite a fall in world commodity prices between 1873 and 1896. In response, the Swedish Sawmills and

Wood Exporters' Association was founded in 1875 in an attempt – tried several times unsuccessfully – to restrict output and maximise prices.

Although the trade from Russia developed later than sales from both Norway and Sweden, the sheer scale of its forests, once utilised, soon had an important influence on the commerce in timber. By the 1860s, exports from Russia and its imperial province, Finland, outstripped those of Norway, and then dislodged Sweden from its premier place as importer to Britain – won in 1873 – within two years. Nonetheless, felling and sawmilling in Russia were primitive by comparison with competitors, and they became dependent upon subcontracting and investment by foreign firms and syndicates, although, as a result, the export trade had achieved significant technical and operational improvements by the First World War. In 1900, the Swedish contribution to European and world exports stood at 34.4 and 21.8 per cent; Russia at 21.9 and 14.9. By 1913, the figures were 25.3 and 16.6 for Sweden, and 35.2 and 23.1 for Russia. Within a decade, then, the respective positions had been almost exactly reversed.[5]

Canada was, incidentally, to regain its place as pre-eminent importer of timber to Britain but not until the Second World War, when Nazi control of Europe and the Baltic sea-routes terminated supplies. This achievement proved a temporary consequence of war.

In the years after 1870, therefore, Britain had to rely on Baltic softwoods, yet it had already begun to look to North America for hardwoods. Supplies were obtained from the southern part of the Austrian Empire – financed by British capital and imported by well-known firms such as Latham's and Mallinson's – but from the 1880s the country began to import considerable quantities of Canadian and American hardwoods. Certainly, timber remained central to the economies of New Brunswick and Quebec, and North America generally benefited from well-developed waterway and railway networks and an efficient sawmilling industry.[6] The modern teak trade – largely from India, Burma, Java and later Siam – was also established during the 19th century. Indeed, the availability of tropical hardwoods from all over the world gradually increased, although they still awaited the fullest exploitation. The plywood business expanded at the same time.

The principle of cross-grained sheets being glued together for enhanced strength had been well understood for many years, but the invention of the rotary knife-cutter in the 1890s allowed large sheets to be produced. Plywood – first used extensively in the manufacture of tea-chests – became within a few decades one of the timber trade's most important products, and the Baltic – endowed with birch forests ideal for the purpose – was the main beneficiary. Other technical developments – modern band-mills with 12 inch blades, better planing machines, and cylindrical cutter-heads for moulding – helped supply keep pace with demand. Technological developments had implications in the consuming countries too: the patenting of creosote and, in the 1890s, the adoption of the first primitive kilns respectively spread wood's applications and sped the process of seasoning, just as band-saws and power-machinery had an impact on their indigenous timber trades and the volumes which they could process.[7]

By 1913, 7 per cent and 8.9 per cent of timber volumes imported into the United Kingdom originated from the United States and Canada respectively; Sweden and Norway accounted for 16.2 and 3.9; but some 48 per cent of all wood came from Russia and Finland.[8] These five countries, therefore, served as Britain's principal suppliers – Norway and Canada for centuries – and all of them had met the unprecedented consumer demand for timber in Britain over some 50 years. The development of the modern trade was by force of circumstances rapid: overseas supplies and trading connections had to be quickly built if the demand for timber – representative of growing living standards at home – was to be fulfilled.

II: TRADE STRUCTURE

But to what purposes was all this timber used, and how was the British timber trade organised? The structure of the industry was determined by its international character, the nature of the commodity and by the differentiated character of demand and final usage. As we have seen, there were a number of different activities involved in the felling, sawing, and exporting of timber overseas. Shippers – not to be confused with the shipowners whose services they purchased – might be involved in forestry and sawmills, but, in many cases, they might purchase timber for cutting or buy it ready-sawn. They would, in general, obtain their supplies from many different sources. Foreign shippers were important players in the world timber trade, partly because, after all, they physically linked international supply and demand, and partly because many of them were comparatively large-scale operations.

Wood, of course, is a natural commodity that grows in non-standard shapes and sizes, and its price was related to the fellers' ability to saw, mould and sell as much of the tree as possible. Exporters – especially those with their own lumber and sawmilling operations – had to be conscious of these cost implications, just as they sought a variety of timber sizes and types to fill fully the ships they commissioned. They needed, therefore, the services of an agent who, located in the destined market, could sell complete timber lots to a list of importers with differing purchase requirements. Agents could also keep overseas shippers informed of the market situation. Both shippers and agents did, of course, concentrate on general areas of the trade such as hardwood, softwood, or plywood, and some operated on a smaller scale in specialist, high value woods like mahogany. But, within broad categories, the varieties of timber types, shapes and qualities could appear infinite, and traders required detailed knowledge of these commodities. The agent worked directly for the shipper and checked each shipment. But, given the need to sell every part of a shipment when landed, the agent maintained close relations with importers and often operated according to a restricted list. Agents also arranged credit. These close links guaranteed sales for the shipper and supplies for the importer, an advantage accentuated by the

Price Walker Saw Mill, Gloucester, c.1900.
Courtesy of Gloucestershire Library, Local Studies.

The conveyance of timber to the roadway from the scene of felling using a wire ropeway with Blonden tackle, Glen Artney.
B.T. Batsford Ltd

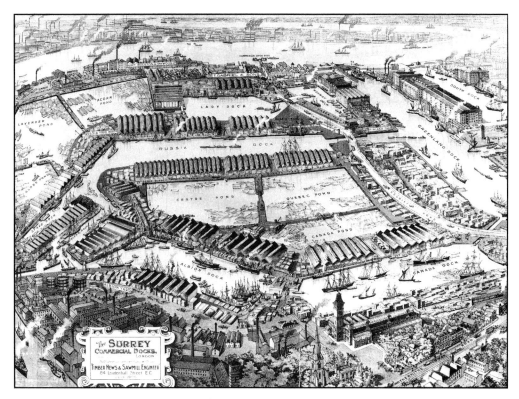

Bird's-eye view of the Surrey Commercial Docks, 1906. Sponsored by 'Timber News & Sawmill Engineer'.
Reproduced by Permission of the Museum in Docklands, PLA Collection, London.

Tayport Harbour, c. 1910.
Courtesy of James Donaldson & Sons Ltd., Fife.

cyclical nature of demand and prices in timber trade. Sometimes, softwood and hardwood agents acted as brokers: while agents acted for shippers and often sold wood unseen, brokers would sell existing and landed stocks.[9]

Importers, having bought consignments of timber through agents, normally stored their purchases in yards or wharves. The larger importers might own sawmilling facilities and undertake their own cutting, but the amount of hewn and round wood imported amounted to less than 10 per cent by volume in the early years of the 20th century (*see* Table III). They could, however, adapt sawn imports to meet the exact requirements of customers. Some were all-purpose importers, but the majority worked in particular trades, most obviously for the building industry. Such importers required good connections with timber merchants located throughout the country, although traders in specialist hardwoods would be more likely to buy according to the specific requirements of end-users and, therefore, would tend to deal directly with them.

The building industry was itself notoriously cyclical. Consequently, its raw material demands varied dramatically over time and the composition and size of each construction task affected the nature of orders, too. Rather than tying up capital in the storage of basic materials like timber, builders preferred to buy their wood from a merchant just before it was needed, just as importers were accustomed to supplying merchants from stock. Only large furniture companies or brewers and millers that made barrels found advantages in buying directly from agents or shippers, a tendency most of the timber trade saw as threatening its structure and, overall, the efficient supply of wood to the majority of users.

But, on the whole, the trade was markedly differentiated by function – chiefly by the roles of shipper, agent, importer, and merchant – due to a variety of product specialisations and because of its worldwide geographical dimensions. Product differentiation encouraged the existence of many, small scale firms, as did the many process stages which timber underwent. In most cases, there were few benefits in terms of transaction costs to be gained from the coordination of timber felling, sawing and distribution. Moreover, the almost universal use of wood necessitated the existence of many small-scale buyers and distributors. Cyclical tendencies in the economy and in the trade also favoured the existence of small, sometimes marginal units, although they responded to this difficulty by close connections, which resulted in many cases in restrictive practices intended to limit the number of firms. Product, geography, and demand worked against any tendency – obvious in other sectors – towards industrial clustering in certain areas, and an absence of vertical or horizontal merger maintained an industry of small, atomistic firms.[10]

The nature of the British timber trade, particularly its reliance on imports and its links with the construction industry, determined its organisation and structure. Much of the imported wood arrived at the Port of London, originally at the larger wharves near Lambeth, latterly at the better-equipped Surrey Commercial Docks. Furthermore, because a large part of the Baltic and North America was ice-bound for 4–5 months of the year, the summer was reserved for receiving and sorting at British docks, and the winter was used for distribution inland. Several large firms emerged at an early date, and they were – not surprisingly – located near ports. James Latham Ltd, for example, was established in Liverpool in 1757 and in London from 1815. Burt, Boulton & Haywood was founded in the metropolis in 1848, and, given the international character of the timber trade, it subsequently set up offices in Paris, Brussels, Bilbao and Riga. But, because the trade acted as a critical link between shippers and the building trade, some timber merchants – like William Marshall of Islington – were founded to meet the needs of growing suburbs and others – such as Jewson & Sons of Norwich – supplied a provincial market.[11]

The bulk of supplies, as we have seen, was destined for the building industry. The welfare and living standards of the nation depended on its ability to be housed, especially as one sign of improvement in the United Kingdom was a rising population: 21m in 1850, 31m in 1870, and 46m in 1913. The British, in addition, became increasingly urbanised: whereas some 50 per cent of the population lived in towns of 20,000 or more inhabitants in 1851, the figure for 1901 was 77 per cent. Cities – particularly London – and suburbs expanded rapidly, and the impact this development had upon the building industry and ancillary trades such as timber was evident. Indeed, building was almost uniquely dependent upon domestic trends and demand – there could be no export trade – and, for this reason in particular, the international trade in timber was linked to living standards and housing.

The general builder and the estate development of homes became dominant: residential building was responsible for 56–60 per cent of all construction in the 40 or so years after 1870 (decennial averages). As a result, employment in the construction industry probably doubled in the 60 years before the First World War. A richer, larger, more urban nation had to be housed, and building attracted investment because the demand for it stemmed from factors such as population size, migration, and age structure, and in many cases continued throughout trade depressions when industrial and overseas investment was discouraged. In the 1870s, building amounted to some 38 per cent of Gross Domestic Capital Formation, and between 1905 and 1914 was still at an approximate level of 30. The industry, furthermore, was slow to use timber-substitutes such as the fully-loaded steel frame and reinforced concrete, the first example being the Ritz Hotel in London in 1904, some 20 years after the USA.[12]

The commerce in timber for furniture similarly expanded, and relied mainly on hardwoods such as mahogany, rosewood and oak. Areas of supply such as the Spanish colonies and North America were long-established, but others in West Africa, India, the Far East, and, in the 20th century, the Japanese island of Hokkaido were soon discovered. The types of hardwood available to the British consumer therefore increased. London was the centre of Britain's furniture industry, perfectly sited for the delivery of timber supplies and sales to the metropolitan market. Furniture makers were responsible in the years before the Great War for about 3 per cent of all timber

Tayport, Ship and Railway, c.1910.
Courtesy of James Donaldson & Sons Ltd., Fife.

The vessel 'Sprightly' in Tayport Harbour, c. 1910.
Courtesy of James Donaldson & Sons Ltd., Fife.

Horse and cart with hardwood log, 1912.
Courtesy of James Latham Plc, Clapton, London.

A horse-drawn sleigh used for timber haulage.
B.T. Batsford Ltd

import volumes, although, in buying a large proportion of expensive hardwoods, it accounted for a far greater part of trade values.

Located at first in the west of the city, furniture firms gradually shifted towards the East End, Shoreditch, Hoxton, Bethnal Green and the Lea Valley; some at the turn of the century were attracted by cheaper land prices and surplus labour to High Wycombe. The industry was transformed from craft to factory production after 1850, and, with the development of plywood in the 1880s and 1890s, it was provided with a cheap material for the mass market. As large numbers of Jewish immigrants arrived in the East End, they brought with them techniques used in the Baltic countries for turning out batch, plywood furniture, and timber importers like Latham's began to supply the unregulated sweatshops established throughout the East End. The firm first entered this business in 1895, having begun as a supplier of mahogany for the furniture industry, and, within five years, the partnership assumed limited liability. Mallinson's, founded in 1877 in Shoreditch, became a pioneer in plywood production in the 1890s, and used its technological knowledge to expand its operations to Rotterdam and Paris.[13]

Some timber firms were closely integrated with regional industries. The City Saw Mills in Glasgow, for example, supplied shipbuilders, and benefited from Admiralty orders during the Great War. James Donaldson & Sons, operating from Tayport, supplied the collieries around Fife. Pitwood was a highly important element in the timber trade – some 11 per cent of all imports by value and 26 per cent of all volumes by 1913 – and the strategical implications of this reliance on overseas sources were all too obvious during the First World War. The commerce in staves – mostly for barrel-making – was much smaller, but not insignificant (*see* Table III). In total, the furniture, box, crate, wagon, stave and barrel industries, and the sawmilling operations which backed them were responsible for 2.5 per cent of Gross Domestic Product and, with 239,000 employees, some 3.3 per cent of the nation's labour force. 78,000 of these workers were to be found in sawmilling, and 92,000 – despite using only 3 per cent of import volumes – in furniture making.[14] The manufacture of wagons and barrels declined during the inter-war period, and was insignificant after 1939. In an effort to undertake the colliery repairs postponed during the war, pitwood remained a substantial business during the 1950s, but the commodity was gradually replaced thereafter by steel props. Nevertheless, the timber-using industries continued to employ some quarter of a million people in the post-war years, assisted in part by the rapid expansion of plywood and plywood products. None of these figures, moreover, account for the numbers working in the importing, wholesale and distribution business, for which there are, historically, no reliable figures (*see* Appendices VI & VII).

Firms within the timber trade, then, were split by function and by variation in the final purpose of the raw material. These divisions between brokers and agents, importers of foreign wood and indigenous timber merchants – and between softwood, hardwood, and, latterly, plywood traders – were deeply rooted, and, as we shall see later, created obstacles to joint cooperation. The presence of the timber trade throughout the country and the existence of local and regional interests and loyalties amplified the difficulties. As we have noted, the need for some unity of purpose was first recognised in the 1890s when the timber trade – a complex network of dealers and merchants engaged in a substantial and vital task – reacted to the political and economic problem of railway rates. For a good that was bulky and by necessity transferred from ports to every part of Britain, transport charges were critical and dominated the actions of the Timber Trade Committee and its successor, the Timber Trade Federation, in its early years (*see* Chapter II). The success with which it protected its interests in the arena of government – sometimes counter to the lobbying of the railways – would, in some respects, be a measure of the importance government attached to the commerce in timber. It would also say much about a trade dominated by small, independent merchants with differing concerns and no tradition of cooperation.

Between the 1860s and the early 1890s, we have seen how the trade encountered few difficulties – it was a period of continuous expansion – and there appeared little reason for joint action. Then, the issue of transport arose as the principal concern of the trade, and remained so until the problems of shipping losses and shortages were encountered between 1914 and 1918. During the inter-war years, the collapse of prices and trade instability drove the industry towards collective action and restrictive practices within functional and product groups and under the aegis of the Timber Trade Federation. Firms sought to protect an industrial structure established during the previous century, yet, after the Second World War, legal restraints placed upon restrictive practices gradually forced them to review questions of organisation and trade representation. Nevertheless, it was clear by the 1890s that the timber trade had a substantial interest to protect. Given the political and public issue of railway monopoly and prices, could it organise effectively?

REFERENCES

1. W. Ashworth, *A Short History of the International Economy since 1850*, 1962, p.182–217; A.G. Kenward & A.L. Lougheed, *The Growth of the International Economy, 1820–1960*, 1971, pp.13–17, 25–30, 90–104; J. Foreman-Peck, *A History of the World Economy*, 1983, pp.33–66, 94–126. Cf. also A. Gerschenkron, *Economic Backwardness in Historical Perspective*, 1962; J.D. Gould, *Economic Growth in History*, 1972; C.P. Kindleberger, *Foreign Trade and the National Economy*, 1962; S. Kuznets, *Economic Growth of Nations: Total Output and Production Structure*, 1971; The Economist, *Economic Statistics, 1900–83*, 1983, p.10.

2. The improvement in the export-import ratio, it should be noted, can be attributed to the particularly favourable circumstances of 1913.

3. Cf. B.R. Mitchell, *British Economic Statistics*, 1990.

4. B. Latham, *Timber: its Development and Distribution*, 1957, pp.39–40, 45, 48–56; *Timber Trades Journal*, 21 Nov 1931.

5. E.F. Soderlund (ed.), *Swedish Timber Exports, 1850–1950: a History of the Swedish Timber Trade*, 1952, pp.3–40, 48–50, 59, 69–130, 170–87, 311–3; J. Ahvenainen, 'Britain as a Buyer of Finnish Saw Timber, 1760–1860' in *Shipping and Trade in the Northern Seas, 1600–1939*, 1988, pp.149–62; Latham, 1957, pp.40, 48, 56–7, 92–104.

6. Latham, 1957, pp.56–60; Soderlund, 1952, pp.106–13, 131–47; L.B. Dixon, *The Birth of the Lumber Industry in British Columbia*, 1956. Cf. also H. Clepper, *Professional Forestry in the United States*, 1971.

7. Latham, 1957, pp.58, 61–2.

8. R. Zon & W.N. Sparhawk, *Forest Resources of the World*, Vol.I, 1923, p.178.

9. B. Latham, *The History of the Timber Trade Federation of the United Kingdom: the First Seventy Years*, 1965, pp.58, 77; Monopolies and Restrictive Practices Commission, *Report on the Supply of Imported Timber*, 1953, pp.3, 10–15; J.H. Leigh, *The Timber Trade: An Introduction to Commercial Aspects*, 1980, pp.12–20.

10. Latham, 1965, pp.58, 77; 1953 Report, pp.3, 10–15, Cf. A.D. Chandler, *The Visible Hand*, 1977, & *Scale and Scope*, 1990; M.E. Porter, *The Competitive Advantage of Nations*, 1990; Leigh, 1980, pp.12–20.

11. Latham, 1957, pp.iii–xv; Latham, 1965, pp.13–14, 17, 19–20, 22.

12. Latham, 1965, pp. 17, 23; H.W. Richardson & D.H. Aldcroft, *Building in the British Economy between the Wars*, 1968, pp.22–31; S.B. Saul, 'Housebuilding in England, 1890–1914', *Economic History Review*, 1962, xv, pp.119–37. Cf. also J. Parry Lewis, *Building Cycles*

and Economic Growth, 1965; B. Thomas, *Migration and Economic Growth*, 1954; H.J. Habbakuk, 'Fluctuations in Housebuilding in Britain and the United States in the 19th Century', *Journal of Economic History*, 1962, vol.xxii, pp.198–230.

13. Latham, 1957, pp.39–40, 62, viii, x, xv; J.L. Oliver, *The Development of and Structure of the Furniture Industry*, 1966, pp.23, 38, 47, 97; W. Hamish Fraser, *The Coming of the Mass Market, 1850–1914*, 1981, pp.197–200; Interview with T.S. Mallinson, 3 October 1991.

14. Census of Production, 1907; James Donaldson & Sons Ltd, *In Their Father's Footsteps*, 1985, p.9; J. Carvel, *One Hundred Years in Timber: the History of the City Saw Mills*, 1949, pp.62–66.

━ II ━
REPRESENTATION AND
TRANSPORT, 1891–1921

I: POLITICS AND THE RAILWAYS

Oｎｅ factor and one alone inspired the founding of the Timber Trade Federation in the 1890s: the anger which the industry's firms, like so many other traders, felt about the raising of railway rates. A high level of concern about these charges was not unreasonable. Despite the existence of canals, coastal shipping and inchoate forms of motorised road transport, railways continued to dominate the movement of goods and passengers in Britain. The rates set by railway companies, therefore, had a critical impact upon every commodity and, ultimately, upon the wider economy.

As dealers in a heavy, natural and non-standardised commodity, timber merchants bore heavy transport costs, and their product – far from being near its point of use – was almost wholly imported and subsequently moved by some means to every part of the country. Rising transport costs particularly affected the price of timber and the profitability of the trade. They, therefore, influenced the fortunes of the building industry, collieries, furniture makers, and other large users of timber. Victorian railway rates were by necessity a question critical to all areas of commerce and the economy, but the debate became particularly highly-charged because they were a political issue too.

Railways had become government-regulated enterprises in this century of *laissez-faire* because they were naturally monopolistic and less affected by the market and price disciplines experienced in other sectors. Many elements discouraged effective rivalry. As quite unprecedented large-scale investments, railways could only be financed as joint stock companies, a form of ownership historically associated with fraud and so illegal before the 1860s without a special Act of Parliament. The complications of obtaining Parliamentary sanctions were a barrier to market entry. In any case, legislation to sanction compulsory purchase was required before the construction of any line, and complicated and expensive official procedures investigated the need for any project. Both the controls on financing and building limited the threat from competitors. The efficient transfer of traffic across the country encouraged networks under the control of one or a few companies, and, as well as being large-scale, railways were also capital-intensive. They consequently required a huge through-put that secured returns on their investment, and, despite notable examples of rivalry, competition between companies often proved wasteful and eventually self-defeating, even if it persisted in many instances. To prevent railways exploiting their monopolistic position, their charges were subjected to governmental scrutiny, and traders had a special interest in the framing of railway legislation and the determination of freight charges.[1]

Why, however, did the issue of railway rates become so problematical in the 1890s? The immediate cause of dispute was the Railways Bill of 1891 which, to the great dissatisfaction of timber and other traders, classified types of freight and the charges that could be levied. Such dissatisfaction had a long history. In the 1820s and 1830s, individual railway company Acts had generally authorised maximum mileage charges based upon use of the track and notions of 'market value', but provision was rarely made for use of locomotives, carriages, and warehouses. Early railway legislation, therefore, was anachronistically influenced by canal practice, where traders would pay for right of passage but remain in charge of their own barges. There was some justification for the law at this time setting only general maximum rates, and not specific charges which could be designated as 'fair'. Canals and shipping, after all, did provide extensive competition to the railways and theoretically kept their rates in check. But the completion of Britain's railway trunk routes by the 1840s supplied the train with an unmatched speed and cost advantage over other forms of transport, although the volumes that continued to be carried by canal and coastal shipping should not be underestimated. Nevertheless, the railways had certain monopolistic advantages, and there was a growing realisation that canals were operationally distinct.

In response, the Railway Act of 1844 empowered the Treasury to reduce the charges of any company earning profits which exceeded 10 per cent on its capital. Any increase in the regulation of the railways, however, was in part stymied during the next two decades by external factors. Just when government became interested in the control and monitoring of railway monopoly, the repeal of the Corn Laws in 1846 caused political divisions which hindered the passing of controversial or complicated legislation. The two party system was replaced by a number of Parliamentary factions whose support for any measure could not be assumed. With voting majorities small and fluctuating, the influence of the 'Railway Interest' – some one hundred or so MPs connected to the industry – was enhanced, and the Railway Companies Association was a comparatively effective representative organisation with well-established Parliamentary connections. There was, on the other hand, little pressure for greater state intervention.

Railways began to expand their services and carry larger volumes of low margin freight, and their rates and profits fell, although antagonism between the companies and traders never disappeared. The establishment of the Railway Clearing House in 1847 systemised rates and the classes of passengers and goods transferred between regional companies, which could as a consequence quote a price for carriage to anywhere in the country. But the process of classifying goods according to the new national list was a complicated one, and unequal treatment and therefore varying charges continued. Local rates, moreover, were not standardised, and there were still no guidelines on terminal and demurrage charges nor on the thorny question of discounts. High fixed costs were intrinsic to the nature of railway enterprise, and the companies were always willing to offer special rates which could improve marginal revenues. It followed that they offered special discounts to traders seeking to compete in distant markets and to those who might send their goods by canal or coastal shipping. Traders who did not benefit from this discrimination were naturally aggrieved, and in 1854 Parliament did forbid any rates whose differences could not be justified on grounds of cost. Given the complexity of goods classification and the problems of isolating costs, this legislation proved impractical, and throughout the 1850s and 1860s plaintive traders impressed official bodies of enquiry with stories of arbitrariness, secrecy and high handedness. On the other hand, it was the railways which had to cope with the managerial problems of rate-setting, high fixed costs, falling revenues and specific instances of competition. Companies rarely earned a 5 per cent return on their capital – considerably below the legal maximum of 10.[2]

1867 marked a turning-point in railway–state relations. The extension of the franchise in that year brought a limited form of popular representation and so encouraged party political organisation. The ensuing polarisation between Liberals and Conservatives in Parliament weakened the influence of interest groups like the Railway Companies Association. Furthermore, when a Royal Commission in 1867 argued that it was neither practicable nor desirable to control railway rates, its recommendations soon seemed anachronistic. The government, indeed, became increasingly more responsive to the question, and, in the furtherance of public information, the Regulation of Railways Act 1873 made the publication of rates compulsory. This legislation also established a Railway Commission to investigate the reasonableness of terminal charges and the obligations of companies. Changes in the economy, moreover, combined with political circumstances to encourage general concern about railway rates.

Two decades of inflation had facilitated the payment of railway rates fixed according to individual company Acts, but from 1873 there was a general price fall and profit squeeze which lasted over 30 years. The money cost of wood and timber, for example, was nearly halved (see Table II in Chapter I),[3] and timber merchants like other traders became anxious that fixed railway rates should be adjusted. It was, above all, the trend in prices which provoked the political reaction against the level of railway rates, and also hardened opinion against the monopolistic implications of railway amalgamation proposals. General deflation, moreover, coincided with rising operational costs for the railways, and, as a result, rate increases rather than reductions became more likely.

In 1881 and 1882, a House of Commons Select Committee recommended that general principles on all charges – carriage and demurrage – should replace the existing confusion and lack of uniformity, although it dismissed accusations that the industry was generally derelict in its duties. The increasing complexity of the issue was acknowledged too: railway legislation had originally defined four basic categories of goods and 40 or so commodities, but these figures had expanded by the 1880s to seven and 2,753 respectively. Charges – once based upon market value only – took account of a product's fragility and its bulk, and these considerations affected the carriage of timber. The government's efforts to obtain mutual agreement on outstanding questions proved a lamentable failure, and, six years later, the 1888 Railway and Canal Traffic Act appointed a permanent Railway and Canal Commission to which each company had to submit revised classification and rates schemes. When the Board of Trade invited responses to the railways' proposals, it received 4,000 complaints, and subsequent meetings between traders and the companies failed to find agreement. Eventually, the Railway Clearing House scales were imposed on all long-distance carriage, but local and terminal charges, for which there was no uniform system, were a problem that required years to resolve.[4]

In 1891 and 1892, Parliament passed the Railway (Rates and Charges) Order Confirmation Acts, and these from January 1893 enforced new maxima for every type of charge. Many traders remained dissatisfied with the new legislation, and their disquiet soon increased. The railway companies began to impose these rates which, despite being below previous maxima, were in many cases greater than the discounted charges once actually quoted. With their operating costs rising and freight revenues falling, railways wanted to improve net receipts. They accepted that negotiations with traders would have to take place over discounts, but, in setting rates in the future, they naturally wanted to be in a position of bargaining downwards rather than upwards. The government, moreover, remained reluctant to become involved in their commercial and pricing decisions.

In order to prevent monopolistic exploitation, the state had for a long time accepted the need to set 'reasonable' maxima, but wanted no part in determining actual rates. The railways made the mistake, however, of underrating the strength of public reaction, and, in 1893, they reduced the rates they had just raised. They undertook to limit all increases to 5 per cent above levels in force the year before. But the traders recognised this to be a temporary solution, and they sought to widen the remit of the Railway and Canal Commission through legislation which would allow it to arbitrate on 'reasonable' actual charges and not just maxima. Government and Parliament balked at this controversial proposal – the issue of Irish Home Rule presented enough conundrums – and instead passed an Act in 1894 which froze rates at their 'real' levels of December 1892. Nevertheless, this was a rare demonstration of the legislature acting to protect the interests of one group of traders against the activities of another.[5]

It was, therefore, a combination of economic and political circumstances which necessitated in the 1890s the formation of a trade association whose interests were so interwoven with the problem of railway rates. Price and cost trends had forced the railways and traders into oppositional viewpoints: there was little compromise to be found between the need for rate increases and the need for rate reductions. The resultant controversy produced a problem of daunting complexity with long historical roots. The nature of railway operations and the issue of monopolistic pricing did not concern the legislature until the 1840s and, then, political circumstances had inhibited effective action for 30 years. Parliament was subsequently more willing to regulate the railways, and the general fall in prices during the fourth quarter of the 19th century was the most important factor in stirring trader activism. As the nominal value of its goods decreased, industry wanted a review of railway rates, which were fixed by legislation, and the railways underestimated the level and breadth of the concern focused on this issue. The search for consensus in the 1870s and 1880s, however, was revealed as an elusive policy, and it was not until the legislation of 1891 to 1894 that Parliament finally tackled the crucial subject of railway rates.

With the levels of government intervention and the consequences of legislative decision increasing, the need for representation at the Board of Trade and at the Railway and Canal Commission had become important. It is no surprise, therefore, that the Timber Trade Committee – the forerunner of the Federation – was established by the London Chamber of Commerce's Timber Section and a number of other local associations. Timber merchants were anxious that their views about the railway legislation should be heard, and they were prominent throughout the decade in the political and economic debates over rates.

II: THE FOUNDING OF A FEDERATION, 1891–1900

The *ad hoc* Timber Trade Committee was formed on the 3rd December 1891. It was founded on a feeling that the timber trade's views had been completely overlooked during the passage of the 1891 Railway Rates Act. The industry strongly objected to some of the clauses contained in this measure and wanted their repeal, especially as their principles were inserted in that year into nine railway Acts sponsored by individual companies. It was soon evident that the industry would also fail to influence the passage of the 1892 Rates Bill, although the Committee committed itself to the repeal of its objectionable clauses. In the meantime, the new body wanted to prevent the inclusion of similar provisions in further bills, most immediately that being promoted by the North Eastern Railway.

The timber trade reacted strongly to the general railway legislation of 1891–92 because it not only fixed new maximum charges but allowed the carriers to choose between different methods of charging for wood. From January 1893, railways – as well as introducing new rates – could calculate according to the traditional 'measurement weight' or the alternative of 'machine weight'. As in all matters of goods classification, the matter was extremely complicated, and, depending upon the type of wood and its shape, specifications greatly varied. The changes, moreover, generally affected only imported softwoods. The main point was that, under the first method – measurement weight – the circumferences of set lengths of wood were measured, and the trader would be charged on the basis of a calculation which related circumference to approximate weight. This very traditional approach appeared rudimentary, but was a practical solution to the shortage of weighbridges at many stations and depots. Under the second option – machine weight – the timber was actually weighed. Furthermore – and this was the point – measured freight would in future travel as relatively expensive Class I goods, whereas weighed products would be conveyed at the cheaper Class C. There was an assumption, therefore, that measured weight had unreasonably favoured the timber traders. If, as the TTC pointed out, weighbridges were generally unavailable, railways were being given the chance to reclassify timber and charge a higher price for its carriage. The Committee argued, in addition, that weight was not an objective measurement: timber could be wet or dry, and its condition might depend on the covered storage capacity of railway depots and the efficiency of transfer. Lastly, traders could double check the circumference of their loads, but, if weight were to be the criterion, they had to depend on the reliability and honest setting of weighing machines.[6]

The hardwood trade, on the other hand, was more concerned about specific changes in the calculations of measurement weight which, unlike the case of imported softwood, reduced the length of its wood loads deemed to be equal to a ton. Hardwood firms, therefore, initially perceived cost benefits in the introduction of machine weight, even given the shortage of weighbridges. The interests of the home-grown and the log timber businesses were also at variance to those of softwood importers. These divisions automatically hampered all efforts to lobby Sir Michael Hicks-Beach, President of the Board of Trade, who could see both favourable and unfavourable responses amongst timber firms to recent railway legislation. The industry realised that it did not have the power to reverse government legislation.

This weakness was reflected in the Timber Trade Committee's limited objectives. It could not reverse government measures but sought to prevent the objectionable clauses being more widely operated through inclusion in company railway Acts. Precisely because of the poor chances of success, many in the hardwood trade decided at first to support actual over measurement weight. Nevertheless, the TTC achieved a degree of unity by March 1892 over the NER Bill on a platform that sought the end of dual measurement for timber, carriage under Class C rates only, and a calculation of 50 rather than 40 feet per ton for hardwoods. Its proposals were also quickly rejected by the Parliamentary Joint Committee on Railway Rates, and the TTC had to acknowledge its lack of support at Westminster.

When Christopher Furness – an MP associated with the TTC – tried to amend the North Eastern's Bill on the floor of the Commons, so allowing 'measurement weight' at Class C, he was defeated by thirteen votes. But the smallness of the margin hid the opposition of the Board of Trade, which would not let one railway company be penalised by such changes, and argued that the issue would have to be resolved by a general measure. It was evident, too, that the timber trade remained split on the question of goods classification and calculation. As a consequence of its political defeats, the timber trade decided by May to combine behind the issue of measurement weight and accept the need to obtain across-the-board alterations through negotiations with the railways. Despite the passing of the 1891–92 Acts, which had set maximum rates, Hicks-Beach was keen to avoid direct involvement in the controversy and arranged direct negotiations with the Railway Companies Association.[7]

By the end of the year, only one conclusion was possible: every search for redress before Parliamentary Committees and the Board of Trade had been 'defeated all along the line', and direct negotiations with railways had revealed themselves to be 'a source of serious discouragement'. The failure to make any impact on legislation reinforced the determination amongst some members of the trade to organise effectively. On the 14th December 1892, the London and Provincial Timber Trade at its General Meeting called for a properly constituted and fully representative Timber Trade Federation of the United Kingdom. The new organisation, it was declared, would protect and promote the interests of the timber trade; collect and disseminate commercial statistics and information; support or oppose legislation; and, generally, undertake any activity that would forward the trade's prosperity. Because of varying interests and activities in the industry, the difficulties in forming such an association were obvious. The problem was overcome by the founding of separate committees within the Federation, which would oversee the Foreign Timber Importers, Foreign Timber Merchants, English Timber Merchants, and Brokers and Agents. It was these committees which would pursue the objectives of the TTF, either individually or by collectively agreeing to cooperate. But the failure of the Brokers and Agents' Committee to form itself in actuality only highlighted an absent tradition of unity, and within a dozen years the Foreign Importers split into separate National Softwood and Hardwood Importers' Sections.

The position of local timber associations had also to be considered, and the Federation's constitution was based upon the notion that it would promote common interests whilst 'reserving perfect local liberty of action to constituent members'. Not every company, however, had a local association, and it was decided that firms as well as associate groups could join the TTF, where an Executive Committee would represent them. A UK Timber Committee was formed as the central coordinating body, but, as the Executive Committee in practice assumed its duties, it was quickly wound up. Samuel Boulton of Burt, Boulton & Haywood was elected as the first president[8], and the offices and small staff of the new Federation were provided by the London Chamber of Commerce. The *Timber Trades Journal* wondered if the federal structure of the new body would maintain rather than overcome old divisions, but it was the price paid for any unitary organisation.[9] The establishment of an organisation was not the same as demonstrating its value and effectiveness. The TTF might have failed – as its predecessor had done – to attract broad support from the trade but for one important occurrence: the railway companies' decision to increase actual rates in January 1893.

Indeed, the industry had felt somewhat isolated during its battle over timber rate classification and calculation rates. It had faced an adamant government and the better organised Railway Companies Association. In 1893, its campaign entered a new phase: the timber trade had a more fully representative association, was united by the issue of railway rate rises, and had joined a campaign enveloping a plethora of equally-agitated business groups. By lobbying for a more general cause, the issue of railway charges on all goods, it was given the first real opportunity for success. At the TTF, the Foreign Timber Importers, Foreign Timber Merchants, and English Timber Merchants Committee came together, and protested vigorously in February to the recently-appointed President of the Board of Trade, A.J. Mundella. As we have seen, the government was reluctant to become involved in the setting of actual rates, but, because of widespread protests, it did subject the railways to informal pressure and by March the railways had agreed to negotiate with interested traders.

It was a turning point, for the railways had at first refused to discuss the rate rises with the timber trade, which was aggrieved both at across-the-board increases and at the additional estimated charges of between 18 and 25 per cent that would follow from the designation of wood as a Class 1 good. The TTF, therefore, attended at the Railway Clearing House on the 17th. The railway companies announced their intention to limit all rate increases to 5 per cent, and agreed too that 'measurement weight' at Class C would be applied in the majority of cases. On the other hand, attempts to make them review terminal and demurrage charges for goods which were neither damagable nor covered proved fruitless, and the Federation was concerned that rate changes required only two weeks' notice when its members entered into contracts for six months or a year. Nevertheless, the railways had attracted enough political and public opprobrium to enable the Federation to conclude fairly satisfactory negotiations. But the agreements offered no long-term solution: the railways could always alter their rates and their classification policies at a later date.

It was this problem which a Parliamentary Select Committee had to consider in 1893, and Boulton on behalf of the TTF took the chance to offer his views. He wanted all rate changes to be subject to conciliation and independent arbitration procedures, and stated that, in raising rates, 'it seemed as if the railway companies had really gone off their heads'. While traders could not challenge the legality of what happened, increases, he contended, had been 'unreasonable' and damaging to country's commerce. Like other businessmen, Boulton wanted a more powerful Railway and Canal Commission which could adjudicate between carriers and freight owners and more effectively protect the interests of traders.[10]

It was a suggestion enjoying broad support, but the government rejected it – it was still not willing to be involved in the setting of rates – and, instead, decided upon an Act that fixed rates at the levels current in December 1892. Widespread political reaction, therefore, had enabled the Federation and other traders to achieve a redress of grievances arising from the overall rates increases. But on the question of weighing timber for freight and its eventual classification, the TTF stood alone. Both the Select Committee and the government dismissed the Federation's demand that the law on 'measurement' and 'machine weight' be altered. Nor, despite subsequent meetings at the Railway Clearing House, would the carriers accept statutory confirmation of matters already agreed to voluntarily.

The Federation, in response, helped draft and promote an Amendment Bill, which was introduced by Christopher Furness and seven other sympathetic MPs. The proposal sought to amend the 'evils' caused by practical reclassification under the 1891 and 1892 Acts, and timber companies all over the country were asked to lobby their Parliamentary representatives. But it was too late in the session, and the bill was unable to proceed. Nonetheless, the TTF claimed to have lobbied 200 MPs and, with the help of a friendly Member – Sir Albert Rollit, President of the London Chamber of Commerce – it did reach a compromise with certain canal companies. Both sides agreed to legislation enforcing 'machine weight' at mutually acceptable rates, yet the fact that the canal companies were willing to be a party to a statutory settlement only intensified animus against the railways.[11]

By 1894, therefore, the Timber Trade Federation had been left with one chief preoccupation: to enshrine in law the practices affecting the carriage of wood. In March, the railway companies once more explicitly refused to countenance the suggestion, and failed to meet further complaints. Many of them took the view that legislation and the voluntary agreement of the previous year meant that timber should be 'measured' for weight according to 'tape over' rather than 'tape-under-bark', and were choosing to charge according to the former method. Arguments over demurrage and terminal charges also continued. The companies did agree, however, that details of timber rates should be published in a comprehensive booklet.

Negotiations were still taking place in 1896, and there was as yet no prospect of an agreement. The Federation did marshal complaints about instances of arbitrary or varying practices in the charging of timber freight, and helped to present them to the Railway and Canal Commission. But it was handicapped by the fact that many merchants were not members, and, more crucially, by the fact that a number of traders did not abide by Federation policy and merely accepted 'tape-over-bark' calculations. The matter was not settled until 1901 when the Railway Commissioners considered a case between the Midland Counties Timber Merchants' Association and the Great Western and London North Western Railways. They decided on 'tape-over-bark', but ordered that the 'measurement weight' calculation should be more generous to the traders.[12] Therefore, some compromise was finally achieved, but relations were far from amicable.

Naturally, the Timber Trade Federation – formed to fight on the issue of railway rates – became involved in other industry matters. As early as 1893, the TTF was urging timber merchants to resist local councils like the Cardiff Corporation which wanted to include 'fair wage' clauses in all contracts made with suppliers. Legislation just passed by the Liberal government had set minimum pay levels for council employees, and empowered local authorities to refuse business with firms deemed to be underpaying their workforces. By 1894, the Federation was also supporting legal action against local councils which attempted to classify timber as 'extraordinary traffic'. As a result of such a decision, wood would bear an additional charge for particular damage to the highways. Further protests were lodged against councils passing by-laws requiring timber wagons to carry night lights on loads as well as vehicles. The TTF viewed the idea as discriminatory. When a divisional court in 1895 decided that the requirement was a reasonable one, the Federation backed attempts by Batly Langley and Sir Thomas Roe – MPs 'connected with the Federation' – to outlaw it. The measured failed, but an attempt in the 1897 Vehicles (Lights) Bill to give Parliamentary sanction to by-laws was defeated. By then, Home Office returns showed that 29 county and 18 borough councils treated timber wagons differently.[13]

In short, the Federation was forced during the 1890s to extend its activities from Parliament to other levels of political decision-making. It became aware, moreover, that its concern about the powerful business groups created by railway monopoly was equally applicable in the case of shipping companies which brought timber from all over the world. The contacts between shipowners were undoubtedly close, and they organised 'rings' and pooling agreements covering pricing and routes. They were, furthermore, represented through the well-organised Shipping Federation and the Chamber of Shipping.[14] Individual timber importers undoubtedly saw themselves at a disadvantage when drawing up charter parties which set the terms for the passage of freight.

They were not alone, and in 1895 the TTF supported the Merchant Freighters' Association which was newly-formed and charged with obtaining a better deal from shipowners. In order to pursue the issue, the Brokers and Agents Committee finally constituted itself, and, with the help of its expertise, the Federation began directly to negotiate with the Chamber of Shipping. It then wrote and sold to its members model charter parties which were acceptable to the shipowners and avoided misunderstanding and legal pitfalls. By the end of the 1890s, these agreements covered North Europe, the Baltic, the White Sea, Scandinavia, the North Atlantic and other important areas of timber trade.[15] The TTF was also able to offer its members a model contract with a recommended insurance company, which would deal with payments under the Workmen's Compensation Act 1897. Like other employers, the Federation objected to the increased employment costs under the legislation, and to the ending of private accident schemes previously allowed by the right to 'contract out' of legislation.[16] Despite the lobbying, no case of 'fair wages', 'extraordinary traffic', or special night lights was reversed, but the Federation did develop the traditional functions of a trade

Steam vehicle of the Chawley Timber Brick & Tile Co. Removing home grown timber from the Earl of Abingdon Estates, c.1900.
Courtesy of Timbmet, Oxford.

Loading spruce poles beside a tramway using a Canadian jammer black mount, Argyll.
B.T. Batsford Ltd

association by establishing best or uniform practice, specifically in matters of charter parties and accident insurance policies.

On the core issue of railway rates, the TTF had fortuitously benefited from a general political campaign and, along with other traders, obtained a revision and freezing of charges. It used the opportunity, moreover, to gain in most cases 'measurement weight' at Class C, but failed to win on this point the same sort of legislative protection guaranteeing general rates. Nevertheless, the Timber Trade Federation could claim to have had a useful, necessary purpose and a fair measure of success. Despite great concern about railway rates during the 1890s, it might seem curious that, although a number of key issues remained, this preoccupation faded after 1900. In fact, the answer was quite straightforward: just as the existence of railway rates fixed in law had for the final quarter of the 19th century aggrieved traders facing falling prices and revenues, so rising prices and revenues after 1900 benefited the self-same traders and, this time, disadvantaged railways subject to set rates. Changes in the economic cycle meant that rates and their revision emerged as a problematic issue for the railway companies. It was, ironically, traders who began to oppose any alteration of the 1894 Act, and they accordingly dropped their calls for the Railway and Canal Commission to supervise and amend charges. With the problem of railway rates no longer pressing, the TTF had lost its main cause for being.

III: PORT MONOPOLY AND TIMBER SUPPLIES, 1900–1921

The TTF was soon drawn into other issues which impinged upon the interests of timber importers and merchants. These were linked, once more, to questions of transport monopoly – not the railways, on this occasion, but the docks. London could not cope with its sea-borne trade, nor accommodate the larger steamships. The port was dominated by one major amalgamated concern which owned the London, St Katharine, East India, West India, Albert and Tilbury docks. But it faced competition from independent wharfingers and lightermen who did not bear the costs of docks and sorting sheds. Following the repeal of protective duties in the mid-19th century, importers no longer had to place their goods in the bonded warehouses owned by the ports, and they – not surprisingly – increasingly offered their business to the cheaper wharfingers and lightermen. London's dock companies were compelled to lower their unloading charges, and their falling profitability made any large-scale modernisation of the port impossible and threatened the capital's position as a trading centre. Like other traders, timber importers were impeded by the inefficiencies of the port system at London. But the dock companies aroused opposition in 1900 when they sponsored a Bill proposing further amalgamations and seeking the imposition of a toll on all goods and on the use of lightermen's barges. A larger concern, it was suggested, might direct the port's affairs more effectively, and the greater revenues would ensure that every user contributed to the up-keep and development of facilities. On the other hand, shippers and importers quickly objected to proposals which would raise tolls and directly increase their costs, and the Bill was withdrawn. But some solution had to be found to the organisational difficulties of London's port, and the government decided to appoint a Royal Commission.[17]

The TTF had in 1900 already formed a London Section, and it was this new body which organised the giving of evidence before the Royal Commission. The Federation was keen to cooperate with the London Chamber of Commerce, but, with one tenth of foreign tonnage imported into the metropolis being timber, it believed its interests were under-represented there. The Commission reported in 1902, and decided upon a single, statutory Port of London Authority. In this instance, competitive private enterprise was adjudged a failure. As soon as a government Bill was presented – in 1903 – the TTF argued for representation on the proposed Authority, but was rebuffed. It was particularly worried by new powers to impose port dues on goods and, at the Surrey Commercial docks, by suggested levies on shipping. The Surrey docks, one of the world's largest timber-importing centres, handled softwood from Sweden, Norway, Finland, and Russia, and pine and spruce from Eastern Canada and Oregon. Hardwoods such as mahogany from British Honduras, Nicaragua, Cuba, Costa Rica, and West Africa, as well as cedar, walnut, rosewood, ebony, boxwood and teak went in the main to the West India docks. In response the Federation separately petitioned against the London Port Bill, and moved a number of Parliamentary amendments. It was worried that, although a unitary authority would provide coordination and adequate investment, the resulting monopoly might have hidden dangers. So, the TTF wanted representation on the suggested Authority, or, alternatively, consultation on appointments. It sought, too, a right of appeal to the Railway and Canal Commission in the event of disputes over charges.

All the TTF's amendments failed, but the Board of Trade did give assurances about 'reasonable' charges and recognised the Federation as the representative body on all timber matters at the port. But Ion Hamilton Benn, a member of the London County Council and chairman of the TTF's London Section, complained of the trade's apathy to the Port of London Authority Bill in 1908, when it became law. The Federation was reported as fairly satisfied with the legislation, having been given assurances that the PLA would be monitored by the Board of Trade. The Authority was officially established in 1909, and, as soon as it published its mandatory schedule of maximum prices, the TTF – led by Hamilton Benn – lodged objections. The London timber trade complained about paying higher rates than users of outports, and, while accepting the PLA's need for increased revenues, it argued that they were carrying a disproportionate burden. The Board of Trade held a public enquiry into the PLA's charges in 1910, but at the suggestion of the London Chamber of Commerce it was dissolved into direct negotiations between specific importers and the Authority. These separate conferences, however, failed to find a solution which satisfied the TTF.[18]

It was no coincidence that the timber trade was heavily involved in the economic and political controversies of transport policy. This entanglement was inevitable because of the nature and structure of the industry. As we have seen, Britain was dependent upon imported supplies of foreign timber which, having arrived at the ports, were moved all over the country. Transport questions were integral to the day-to-day concerns of timber merchants and the TTF, yet the nature and structure of the trade created an additional problem. Because Britain obtained an essential raw material like timber from abroad, there were strategic concerns about national dependency and the neglect of indigenous forests. In truth, the issue did not develop into a major difficulty until the country was threatened by Germany's submarine campaign during the Great War, a conflict of unprecedented magnitude that challenged many assumptions and traditional approaches. But, by the turn of the century, the government was forced to assess the way in which Britain had met its economic needs by mass imports for over 50 years, and to consider the importance of timber as a raw material.

Anxiety about the depletion of Britain's forests had been expressed throughout the 19th century, and public enquiries were held into the management of Crown lands in 1833, 1848, and 1863. But the strategic and economic implications of inadequate forestry resources were not fully considered until a Parliamentary Select Committee investigated the problem between 1885 and 1887. The English Timber Section of the TTF was naturally interested in the development of home-grown supplies, and in 1902 presented evidence to a Departmental Committee at the Board of Trade, appointed 'to enquire and report as to the present position, and future prospects of forestry, and the planting and management of woodlands in Great Britain'. It concluded that indigenous forestry had been neglected, and argued that two areas of approximately 2–10,000 acres each should be cultivated in Hampshire and near Edinburgh. It sought, in addition, educational and training initiatives in forestry skills.

Contemporaneous with the Departmental Committee, a Royal Commission investigated the strategic implications of Britain's dependence on imported supplies, but, despite its awareness of submarine warfare and the power of modern armaments, the position was judged to be secure. It was a view that held even after the Russo-Japanese War of 1904–5, when Russia's Pacific fleet was badly damaged and its Baltic fleet destroyed. Changes in forestry policy did occur, but not for strategic or naval reasons. When Lloyd George presented his 'People's Budget' of 1909, he provided funds for the exploitation of natural resources like woodlands. It formed part of the Liberal government's policy to alleviate poverty and unemployment through pensions, National Health and Unemployment Insurance, labour exchanges, and the financing of necessary development schemes and afforestation during periods of depression. Interestingly, Ion Hamilton Benn MP protested on behalf of the TTF at the inclusion of sawmills amongst those in the unemployment insurance scheme. More to the point, the fiscal consequences of the Liberals' programme – graduated income and special property taxes – were viewed as discriminatory by a Conservative-dominated House of Lords, which decided to resist Lloyd George's proposals. After a constitutional crisis and the passing of a Parliamentary Bill that curbed the powers of the Upper House, the 1909 Budget was finally passed in 1910. It was not until 1911, therefore, that the Development Commission and its Forestry Committee were established and began to allocate grants for training and planting.[19]

But the expenditure on indigenous forests remained minimal compared to the scale of the whole timber trade. Woodlands in the UK continued to be depleted at a rate of 1,000 acres per annum, and by 1913 stood at 3m acres or about 4 per cent of the nation's entire land area. On the other hand, there was little anxiety when war broke out in 1914, because stocks were high and it was not anticipated that the conflict would be long-lasting. When Montague Meyer – a member of a prominent trade firm – was appointed Timber Buyer for every government department in 1914, there was no plan to control imports of the raw material. There was, however, some initial concern about pitwood – it being crucial to the maintenance of coal output – but the newly-created Pitwood Department at the Board of Trade conducted a survey which discovered supplies of eighteen months to two years.

Until May 1915, imported timber tonnage was sustained at 75 per cent of the pre-War average, but an effective submarine campaign quickly began to have an impact. As a result, the President of the Board of Agriculture, Lord Selbourne, in November appointed F.D. Acland MP as chairman of a Home-Grown Timber Committee with a remit to develop domestic resources. The government was also determined to restrict unnecessary usage and save valuable shipping space, moreover, because wood was important to the defensive constructions and trenches which stretched along the Western Front, and it wanted to ensure priority for the armed services. There was criticism, too, that traders had taken advantage of the situation and raised prices to unfair levels. The Committee also designated mill sawyers, timber carters, hauliers and wood fellers as 'reserved occupations' and so prohibited conscription or transfer from these crucial jobs to the Army and other industries. As domestic output increased, the established British sawmills could not cope with the needed volumes, and the Committee founded its own establishments. In January 1916, the government forbade the import of hardwoods, furniture woods and veneers without a Board of Trade licence, and, in March, the limitation was extended to furniture and other wood manufactures. By December 1916, the Home-Grown Timber Committee's enterprises had despatched some 0.2m cubic metres of domestic wood, but the smallness of this contribution was evident, especially in the new year when the shipping and import position in all commodities had worsened, and general rationing and controls had to be tightened. Government administrative machinery was re-organised to meet a growing emergency: the Home-Grown Timber Committee was wound up, and its duties were transferred in March to a Directorate of Timber Supplies at the War Office, which had control over both indigenous and foreign supplies. The Directorate broke the home industry into geographical divisions, each with its own staff for felling, transport and conversion.[20]

Within a short time, the seriousness of the supply position forced the government to involve itself directly in the sale of all timber. The state already controlled a large part of British forestry and overseas purchase and importation, and, consequently, the volume of timber consumed. But, as increasingly limited supplies caused inflationary pressures, it was compelled to institute price control. The government having assumed a wider role in the industry, responsibility for it had to be moved from the War Office to a Timber Supply Department at the Board of Trade. Control of the product ceased to be merely a military matter and became one with general economic implications. To extend controls in 1917, the Board commonly relied on businessmen with experience in a relevant trade, and, likewise, appointed Sir James Ball – a railway and civil engineer with experience of docks construction – to be Controller of Timber Supplies. After 1917, restrictions on speculative stocking, the felling of wood without a licence, and most imports were imposed or improved, as were controls over the use of wood as fuel and on the movement of pitwood. By April 1917, the price of timber was frozen and purchase was limited to national or urgent civil needs. The Timber Trade Federation, however, held a meeting in October 1917 to protest against this growing incidence of state control, and complained at the lack of consultation. Attended by four hundred people, this amounted to at that date the TTF's largest gathering. It feared permanent damage to the timber trade and the prospect of controls continuing after the war. Recent emergency measures seemed to imply, furthermore, that the trade had failed to meet the country's wartime needs. James Ball met these grievances by appointing a Merchants' Advisory Committee for imports and a Home-Grown Timber Merchants' Committee to advise his department. The TTF felt that its expertise and position as the representative organisation of the timber trades had been overlooked by the government for over two years.[21]

As the state became more involved in the economy, it needed to improve its contacts with industry and their representatives. The new government departments being created needed experienced staff and the cooperation of businessmen and managers. There had seemed little reason for a national trade association until, under government encouragement, the Federation of British Industries was formed in 1916, just as the state was instrumental during 1917 in establishing the National Federation of Iron and Steel Manufacturers.[22] The creation of a controlled economy after nearly three years of war was a consequence of submarine warfare and the shipping shortage. *Laissez-faire* and 'business as usual' could not rally the country's resources behind a concerted war-effort. Therefore, it is not surprising that the state overlooked the Timber Trade Federation until 1917 and simply imposed measures of control. But, although industry was increasingly consulted, government continued to set the agenda: better contacts merely made the implementation of decisions more effective and facilitated the flow of information between Whitehall and the world of business. It was by no means inevitable that all restrictions would be terminated with the end of the war. For one, supply shortages might continue, and some examples of central economic planning had brought benefits that might possibly be retained after the cessation of hostilities. Moreover, the morale of the armed forces and the civilian population had to be sustained, and a Ministry of Reconstruction began in 1917 to draw up plans for a better post-war British society. Like many traders, therefore, the TTF became anxious about the continuation of controls and pressed for their end at the earliest practicable moment. It had some grounds for suspicion, because housing was central to Reconstruction plans, and government was considering the retention of controls over the building industry. Raw materials and labour would have to be directed if a national housing scheme was to be made a reality.[23]

How effective, however, had government controls been? In particular, to what extent had they minimised the import of foreign timber? The impact of controls in 1917–18 and – with the exception of pitwood restrictions – their lifting in March 1919 can be seen (*see* Appendix III). The real value of timber imports fell from the beginning of the war, and declined to a low point in 1917–18. Even a brief recovery during the two subsequent years did not return imports to pre-war levels, and 1921, of course, marked the beginning of a severe economic depression. There is no doubt, therefore, that the profitability of the timber trade had been damaged during the Great War, and, as a consequence, the TTF was anxious to return to pre-war conditions. Despite the liberalisation of the timber trade by March 1919, the war continued to have repercussions. To satisfy the demand for wood, some 450,000 of the 4m acres of woodland had been depleted, and in September a Forestry Commission was re-appointed to fulfil the Acland Report, published two years previously. The Commission was given the task of planting in 2m acres of pasture land, which, it was believed, could be developed without substantially affecting meat supplies. But its grants were drastically cut, along with many areas of government expenditure, by the 'Geddes Axe' of 1921, though the Commission did receive some extra finance from the Ministry of Labour's Unemployment Fund. The squeeze on expenditure represented a traditional response to the economic depression of that year, and also an abandonment of most Reconstruction promises. The Coalition government's Housing Act was a notable casuality, and, by 1921, the economy was fully decontrolled. Nonetheless, after ten years of existence, the Commission owned some 310,000 acres, only 62,000 short of the Acland plan, and employed approximately 3,000, not including those occupied in Ministry of Labour schemes.[24]

IV: THE EFFECTIVENESS OF TRADE REPRESENTATION

By 1921, therefore, the Timber Trade Federation had involved itself in a number of issues, but had been chiefly concerned with railway rates and classification, the Port of London, and the maintenance of supplies during the war. Nonetheless many of the circumstances which had created great controversies or difficulties out of these issues had altered. The debate over the capital's docks had been in the most part resolved, and 1921 brought the Railway Act intended to balance the interests of shareholders, labour, traders and passengers. The economy, however, was decontrolled, and the government no longer had a need for such close contact with well-organised representative associations like the Federation of British Industries and the TTF (*see* above). Some 30 years after its founding, the Federation needed to reassess its role. This was not a problem easily solved. But how successfully had the TTF achieved its objectives as a trade association over three decades?

Trade associations, of course, have a plethora of purposes, but, for the sake of argument, two broad objectives: one external, namely the need to influence government policy, and the other internal, specifically the improvement of intra-industry organisation. As the timber industry was composed of many small, non-unionised firms, we will ignore the general area of employers' associations and collective bargaining. With regard to trade association's external or political role, there was a long history. The Railway Companies Association or its predecessor had been active since the 1830s, and further associations lobbied Parliament over legislation affecting textile mills, collieries, chemical firms, and trade treaties between the 1840s and 1860s. Certain groups worked on behalf of tariff reform from the 1870s onwards, but this was a measure with the potential to divide rather than unite industry and trade.

Between 1914 and 1921, the involvement of many businessmen in various economic ministries – some of them newly-created under emergency to run the war economy – appeared to open links between the political and business worlds. Some, looking at supposed German practice of industry-wide organisations working with the state in a coordinated export drive, argued for the incorporation of industry and commerce into government as a means of sustaining and promoting British economic advantage. But, as we have seen, both government and mainstream opinion in business abandoned corporatism and the more ambitious plans for state planning in industry by 1921. The implementation of tariffs drew several trade associations back to the political arena in the 1930s, but the level of involvement not surprisingly grew exponentially with the establishment of a controlled economy in the Second World War. But, by the 1950s, government-business relations had returned to their minimalist position, although there were several none-too-committed attempts to formulate an industrial strategy in the 1960s. Pay and incomes policies also drew business into the world of Whitehall, but none or few trade associations or companies felt they exercised any control over such matters.[25]

There are many ways of interpreting business-state relations. Marxist belief sees government in capitalist societies as dominated by those who own the means of production, distribution and exchange. Alternatively, the Pluralist model views the state as open to the influence of many or all interest groups, though corporatism would give special priority to business and trade unions. In all these cases, representative organisations are a crucial element in the country's political economy, an essential part of a coordinated political, economic, and social system within which roles are fairly well defined. There has, however, been one striking feature of relations between trade associations and government in Britain: their lack of systematic organisation and ineffectiveness compared to some other countries. Neither the Marxist nor the corporatist models, despite the breadth of support for the second interpretation, appear adequate. But the pure Pluralist view of interest groups mediating between industry and society and having an important influence on government does not quite fit the evidence either. Although, historically, British government has all too obviously been open to lobbying and political pressures, sometimes to an important degree, a system based on party politics, electoral influences, administrative pressures, personal ambitions, and, on occasions, limited choices, seems also to have had its own priorities, and these have at times overridden the ambitions of interest groups. For this reason, politicians could, if it were convenient, ignore the representations and protests of business, and the success of and support for trades associations seems to have depended on the extent to which they were accepted into political decision-making. When government required the services of trades associations – as they did during both World Wars – it consulted them and had a determinant impact on their effectiveness. Otherwise, the political role of trades associations was heavily constrained. As the Devlin Commission on Industrial Representation was to report in the 1960s: 'All executive policy and most legislation is conceived, drafted and all but enacted in Whitehall.'[26]

To what extent has the general position of trade associations been reflected in the history of the Timber Trade Federation between 1892–1921? Certainly, its predecessor the Timber Trade Committee recognised its lack of political clout during 1892: there was little likelihood of reversing the Railway Rates Act of 1891 and little prospect of stimying the 1892 Bill. So, it concentrated upon changing clauses in individual company legislation, but still without much effect. The TTF was, as we have acknowledged, fortunate that, soon after its founding in December 1892, the railways announced rates revisions which provoked widespread opposition. One of the reasons why British business generally failed to influence government policy was the division of interests between industries and companies. This problem evinced itself in the timber trade, and continued to do so. The rates controversy of 1893 is a rare example of unified reaction amongst a large number of British business interests, because the issue affected them all, although their opposition was, of course, itself directed against a specific business interest. As a result, the government was forced to implement legislative changes, yet the Federation's own success depended on the general nature of the controversy, and it found itself in a weaker position when negotiating with the railway companies for the rest of the 1890s. The TTF, nonetheless, was born out of the railways issue, and was able to represent the trade's view on the Port of London Authority Act. On the other hand, the state during the First World War perceived timber as a strategic resource and so gradually took control of the commodity without really consulting the TTF or its members, which believed that their interests had been simply overlooked.[27]

What advantages, then, did the Federation offer in the way of improved intra-industry organisation? As voluntary bodies, trade associations had to attract members by supplying services best provided on a joint basis. Clearly, some representative organisation was needed to state the trade's views on railway legislation to the government in the 1890s. Some body was additionally required in negotiations with the railway companies, and the London Section of the TTF was recognised as representative of a genuine interest during the passing of the Port of London Authority Act. Much of the Federation's work was, moreover, less public: the standardisation of charter parties and bills of lading – following direct talks with shipping companies – was an obvious benefit to a trade so dependent upon imports. Its advice over workmen's insurance was another example of a useful central service. The exchange and dissemination of information brought obvious if unquantifiable benefits.

There was one other element of intra-industry organisation which a trade association, because of Britain's particular legal framework, could supply: price control and restrictive practices. Instances of this phenomenon were common in Britain, and resulted in some cases from a failure to rationalise industrial structures and from an attempt to substitute returns-to-scale. But it was probably a symptom of many, deep-rooted problems in British industry and was not itself a brake on merger activity. In other cases, like the timber trades, technological and demand factors did not favour oligopoly. Even so, price controls and restrictive practices had a long history in all sectors, and were encouraged by the shortage of supplies and by pooling arrangements during the First World War. It was the economic difficulties of the inter-war period which promoted restrictive practices – but not price collusion – in the timber trade, and it was this issue, along with the housing boom of the 1930s and the controls imposed during the Second World War, which came to dominate the industry's history.[28]

REFERENCES

1. Cf. H. Parris, *Government and the Railways in Nineteenth Century Britain*, 1965; G. Alderman, *The Railway Interest*,1973; R. Fitzgerald *British Labour Management and Industrial Welfare, 1846–1939*, 1988, pp.25–30.

2. Ibid.; P.S. Bagwell, *The Railway Clearing House in the British Economy, 1842–1922*, 1968; P.J. Cain, 'Traders Versus Railways and the Genesis of the Railway and Canal Traffic Act of 1894', *Jl. of T.H.*, 1973, vol.II, pp.65–84.

3. Cf. B.R. Mitchell, *British Historical Statistics*, 1990.

4. Parris, 1965; Alderman, 1973; Fitzgerald, 1988; Bagwell, 1968; Cain, 1973, pp.65–84; T. Gourvish, *Railways and the British Economy, 1830–1914*, 1980.

5. Ibid. Cf. also R.J. Irving, 'The Profitability and Performance of British Railways, 1870–1914', *Ec.H.R.*, 1978, vol31, pp.46–66.

6. Timber Trade Federation, *Annual Report for 1893*, pp.6–8, 12–14; *Timber Trades Journal*, 6 Jan 1892, p.46; 9 Jan 1892, pp.40–1; 21 Jan 1892, p.12; 20 Feb 1892, p.100; 13 Feb 1892, p.137; 12 March 1892, pp.428–9; 13 March 1892, pp.452–3; 25 March 1892, p.479; 30 April 1892, p.598.

7. Timber Trade Federation, *Annual Report for 1893*, pp.6–8, 12–14; *Timber Trades Journal*, 14 May 1892, p.650; 18 June 1892, p.779.

8. Samuel Bagster Boulton (later Sir) was a founder director of Burt, Boulton and Hayward. He was also chairman of the Dominion Tar and Chemical Company and of the British Australian Timber Co. Ltd. Boulton was prominent in giving evidence to the 1892 Select Committee on Railway Rates. Cf. *Who Was Who*, 1916–1928; & *Burt, Boulton & Hayward Ltd: A Century of Progress, 1878–1948*, 1949.

9. Latham, 1965, p.14, 24–27; Timber Trade Federation, *Annual Report for 1893*, pp.1–2; *Timber Trades Journal*, 26 Nov 1892, p.516; 17 Dec 1892, pp.576, 578; 7 Nov 1931, pp.372–5; Monopolies and Restrictive Practices Commission, *Report on the Supply of Imported Timber*, 1953, p.19. The UK Timber Committee ceased on the 17th April 1893. The Importers' Section of the TTF divided into the National Softwood Importers' Section and the Hardwood Section in 1904.

10. Latham, 1965, pp.7, 24–27, 33–4; TTF, *Annual Report for 1893*, pp.12–19; *Annual Report for 1894*, p.34; *Timber Trades Journal*, 14 Jan 1893, p.31; 22 July 1893, p.78. The Federation met the railway managers at the Clearing House on the 17 March, 28 March and 28 November 1893.

11. Ibid.

12. TTF, *Annual Report for 1894*, p.6; *Annual Report for 1895*, p.2; *Annual Report for 1896*, pp.10–11; *Annual Report for 1899*, p.5; *Annual Report for 1900*, p.5–6; *Annual Report for 1901*, pp.11–14, 39–40.

13. TTF, *Annual Report for 1893*, p.22; *Annual Report for 1894*, pp.7–9; *Annual Report for 1895*, pp.2, 8, 11; *Annual Report for 1896*, pp.9–10; *Annual Report for 1897*, pp.17–19; *Annual Report for 1899*, p.6; *Annual Report for 1900*, pp.13–16; Latham, 1965, p.28.

14. D.H. Aldcroft, *Studies in British Transport History, 1870–1914*, 1974, pp.80–5.

15. TTF, *Annual Report for 1894*, p.13; *Annual Report for 1895*, p.2; *Annual Report for 1897*, pp.7–9; *Annual Report for 1898*, pp.4–11; *Annual Report for 1900*, pp.4–5; *Annual Report for 1901*, p.2; *Annual Report for 1938*, pp.54–61; *Timber Trades Journal*, 7 Nov 1931, pp.374–5; Latham, 1965, pp.28–29, 32, 37–8.

16. TTF, *Annual Report for 1898*, p.13; Fitzgerald, 1988, pp.215–9.

17. D. Owen, *The River, the Docks, and the Port*, 1900, pp.74–80; 'The Port of London Authority', typescript at BLPES, 1937.

18. TTF, *Annual Report for 1900*, p.15; *Annual Report for 1901*, pp.18–19; *Annual Report for 1903*, pp.9–12; *Annual Report for 1904*, pp.11–12; D. Owen, *The Port of London: Yesterday and Today*, 1927, pp.59–61; Latham, 1965, pp.52–3; *Timber Trades Journal*, 9 May 1908, p.1052; 4 July 1909, p.2; 17 Oct 1908, p.570; 24 Oct 1908, p.612; 13 Feb 1909, pp.310–11.

19. R. Zon & W.N. Sparhawk, *Forest Resources of the World*, Vol. I, p.149–203; Fitzgerald, 1988, pp.220–5; J.R. Hay, *The Origins of the Liberal Welfare Reforms, 1906–1914*, 1977; Latham, 1965, p.57; N.D.G. James, *A History of English Forestry*, 1981, pp.23, 196–206; 207–225; Latham, 1965, pp.62–73.

20. Ibid.; Latham, 1957, p.63.

21. Ibid.; TTF, *Annual Report for 1917*, pp.31–37; Latham, 1957, p.63; *Who Was Who, 1867–1920*.

22. J. Turner, 'Servants of Two Masters: British Trade Associations in the First Half of the Twentieth Century' in H. Yamazaki & M. Miyamoto, *Trade Associations in Business History*, 1988, pp.173–197; Fitzgerald, 1988, pp.212–215.

23. Cf. M. Swenarton, *Homes Fit for Heroes: the Politics and Architecture of Early State Housing in Britain*, 1981.

24. James, 1981, p.210–211, 216–224; G. Ryle, *The Forest Service: the First Forty-Five Years of the Forestry Commission of Great Britain*, 1965, pp.19–49, 237–310. By 1928, only 3m acres were under woodland; by 1939, some 4m; and, by 1978, nearly 5m.

25. Modern Records Centre, Federation of British Industries, Committee Files, MSS 200/F/ 1/1193; TTF, *Annual Report for 1921*, pp.81–85; *Annual Report for 1922*, pp.21–33.

26. Turner in Yamazaki & Miyamoto, 1988, pp.173–197; J. Turner, *Businessmen and Politics*, 1984; Report of the Commission of Inquiry into Industrial and Commercial Representation (Devlin Report), 1972, p.5.

27. Cf. S. Blank, *Government and Industry in Britain*, 1973; W. Grant & D. Marsh, *The C.B.I.*, 1977; A. Bentley, *The Process of Government*, 1908; C.E. Lindblohm, *Politics and Markets*, 1973; R. Miliband, *The State in Capitalist Society*, 1973; G.K. Wilson, *Business and Politics: A Comparative Introduction*, 1990; K. Middlemass, *Politics in Industrial Society*, 1979, & *Power, Competition and the State*, vols I–III, 1986–1991; N. Poulantzas, 'The problem of the capitalist state', *New Left Review*, vol.58, 1969.

28. Cf. Political & Economic Planning, *Industrial Trade Associations*, 1935; M. Olsen, *The Logic of Collective Action*, 1968; J.P. Nettl, 'Consensus of elite domination: the case of business', *Political Studies*, vol.13, 1965, pp.22–44; R.H. Salisbury, 'An exchange theory of interest groups' in *Interest Group Politics in America*, 1970; Devlin Report, 1972.

—III—

RECESSION, HOUSING
AND WAR, 1922–1952

I: OLD PROBLEMS AND NEW
CONDITIONS, 1922–1929

As wood was imported from all over the world to every part of Britain, it is not surprising that issues of transport – notably railways, shipping contracts, and the Port of London – emerged as an overriding concern of the timber trade and its representative federation in the years before the First World War. It is equally unsurprising that the strategic implications of this dependency upon foreign timber had to be addressed during the Great War and that import and consumption controls greatly affected those involved in this basic commodity. As we have seen (*see* Chapter II, Tables I & II), the value and quantity of timber imports declined sharply between 1913 and 1918; then, despite the lifting of government controls on wood in 1919, they failed to recover by 1920; and fell in 1921 as a result of economic depression. Nevertheless, the ending of war-time controls seemingly proffered a return to 'normal' trading conditions and – at some point in the future – levels of timber sales comparable with pre-war figures. It also released the Federation from its anxieties over government interference, and the organisation began to concern itself with old, traditional problems like transport and railway rates. But circumstances had changed. The year of 1921 marked a change in the industry's history, for, although the railways did resurface as a core issue in the next decade, new conditions prevented them having their previous impact upon the trade and politics of timber.

A number of factors brought these change of circumstances. Undoubtedly, timber volumes by 1924 matched the 1913 level, and, by 1925, the value of imports in real terms had finally surpassed the pre-war figure. But, in contrast to the almost continuous growth in timber imports before the outbreak of war (*see* Chapter II), economic conditions afterwards caused recurrent fluctuations in demand (Table 1).

TABLE I

Imports of Timber into the UK in Current and Constant Values (£m), 1921–1938

Year	Current Values	Price Index (1890 = 100)	Constant Values	% of total imports	m³ millions
1913	33.8	90.3	37.4	4.4	16.4
1921	30.0	198.6	15.1	2.8	6.8
1923	47.7	148.9	32.0	4.4	14.6
1924	51.1	143.1	35.7	4.0	16.4
1930	45.3	118.8	38.1	4.3	14.5
1933	31.7	89.6	35.4	4.7	13.8
1938	46.2	89.4	51.7	5.0	12.2

Source: Appendix III.

Moreover, changes in the nature of demand for wood accentuated difficulties of economic instability in the 1920s. In the aftermath of the Great War, timber was in short supply, but the resources of the steel and cement industries were ample. Many builders, therefore, began to employ alternatives to timber and bricks, and, finding them in many instances more efficient and cheaper, continued to use them. Light steel house-frames protected by concrete especially undermined timber-frame construction, and had the advantages of being more rot, fire and pest resistant. Metal window-frames further damaged the demand for wood. The timber industry did begin to manufacture panels and sections for building in certain rural areas, and timber-frame houses strengthened with steel cladding gained some popularity in Scotland, but neither development could combat the threat that substitutes posed to markets. The timber trade proved more adept at adapting to other developments in its business.

The reason why railway rates did not become as highly charged an issue as previously was linked to growth in other forms of transport. The railways faced increasing competition in the 1920s from motorised road vehicles, and timber and other trades, as the Royal Commission on Transport in 1929–1930 pointed out, resorted to lorries. The flexibility and convenience offered by road transport – particularly in medium and short hauls – were obvious advantages. As a result, the number of goods vehicles in Britain doubled between 1919 and 1921 to 128,000; by 1930, it was approximately 350,000; and it was some half a million by 1938. The rate of contraction in railway freight traffic was greatest between 1924 and 1933 – albeit a mixture of competitive alternatives *and* economic depression – and, although there was some revival in the 1930s, the volume of merchandise travelling by train in 1937 still only amounted to 74 per cent of pre-war totals. The timber merchants of

Marlow's at Bury St Edmunds, for example, successfully expanded in the 1930s because it used lorries to carry supplies direct to building sites.[1] The railways had lost their previous dominance, and ceased to operate an effective transport monopoly. The impact this had on their profits was patent, as was the reduced level of interest shown by traders to the issue of railway rates.

But changes in the means by which freight was carried were not foreseen during the passage of the 1921 Railways Act, which set the basic structure and operations of the industry. Therefore, state decontrol of the economy after the war had – ironically, as events were to prove – at least the capacity to haunt the Timber Trade Federation and other traders: the government, which had taken control of the railways during the conflict, wanted to return the network to private enterprise, and proposals threatened to entrench monopoly and increase rates. After 1900, railway revenues had been eroded by rising costs and the unwillingness of both government and Parliament to allow an increase in charges. The industry attempted to meet this difficulty by proposing cost-saving amalgamations, but the idea of larger monopolies was resisted by the House of Commons. By 1913, the case for railway rate revision was finally met, but once again a Royal Commission was appointed to investigate the issue. Its deliberations were interrupted by the outbreak of war, and the industry was placed under the control of the Railway Executive Committee, whose statutory duty was to fulfil the transport needs of the war-effort. Under the Committee, the railways were guaranteed their pre-war profits, and there were no increases in freight rates. Central direction achieved large savings from waggon-pooling and the streamlining of once duplicated services, and, because of these successes, the government reversed its previous policy and was persuaded of the advantages of amalgamation and rationalisation. Even nationalisation was seriously considered, but the whole issue of the railways' structure was so complex and controversial that the Ministry of Transport, created in 1919, was vested with control of the industry until options had been more fully considered. In January 1920, the Railway Rates Advisory Committee advised the Minister to impose higher, more realistic rates, and freight charges were increased by 25, and in some cases 60, per cent. Rates had been kept artificially low during eight years of rapid inflation. In opposing the rises, the Federation of British Industries, which led the business opposition to these rises, had a weak case and on the whole failed to influence government policy.[2]

By 1921, the Prime Minister Lloyd George's reliance upon the Conservative majority in his Coalition government had brought an end to any ambitious Reconstruction schemes. Indeed, the government responded to economic depression by cutting state expenditure and political factors ruled out any prospect of railway nationalisation. The case for consolidation, however, could not be denied, and the Railway Act in that year created four large groupings from twenty-seven companies. So, the London, Midland & Scottish, the London & North Eastern, the Southern, and the Great Western Railway were finally formed between 1923 and 1924. Their rates were governed by a Rates Advisory Committee, which published details of the charges imposed after the war and a scheme of classification. It was intended that the Act should form the basis of a rate-setting structure which would take account of the interests of carriers, traders and passengers, and the Advisory Committee became the forum for negotiations. Just as, before the war, traders' falling and then rising revenues had coloured their attitudes to the fixed rates of railways (*see* Chapter II), so the political agitation which had briefly opposed the charges stipulated in the founding Act faded after the inflationary years of the post-war boom. Competition from motor vehicles and economic depression caused a decline in the number of passengers and total freight travelling by train, and, because railways carried high fixed costs, this disproportionately affected the profitability of lines. The companies' operating ratio increased from 60 to 80 per cent in the inter-war period, and they never achieved the standard revenues allowed and approved under the Act. In fact, the railways responded to these circumstances by reducing their rates and by 1927 freight charges had been cut by some 40 per cent. The unprecedented number of exceptional rates was ironic, because it had been the intention of the 1921 Act to systemise actual rates by setting them at a fair and generally agreed level. The new, negotiated schedule came into force in January 1928.[3] Economic and market factors had combined to defuse the issue of railway rates: depression and competition from road transport – rather than legislation – had forced companies to lower their charges. The Port of London issue had been settled; the necessity for contact with government had passed with the decontrol of the industry; and the railway rate debate gradually lost its central importance. What was the Timber Trade Federation's purpose?

II: TRADE DEVELOPMENTS AND STRUCTURE, 1921–1939

In 1921, the TTF considered matters of organisation, but it remained a federation dependent on the cooperation of disparate interests. The Executive Committee, unable to act on its own initiative, left an *ad hoc* committee with the task of consulting members. It was eventually recommended that the Federation become incorporated, but only the Humber District Section supported the suggestion, and the TTF settled for a mere rules revision in May 1922.[4] The different affiliated groups which composed the Federation were broadly content with the current organisation which left decision-making and activity to them. They were representative of the timber trade's many interests and industrial structure. During the recession of the 1920s, however, it was the timber trade's very structure of agents, brokers, importers and merchants and the relationship between them that were being threatened. More and more firms and shippers were willing to exclude 'middlemen' and so minimise prices. The industry responded by trying to impose restrictive practices which could regulate trading relations, and it attempted to achieve this objective under the supportive auspices of the TTF.

The existence of traditional and mutually beneficial trading relationships and restrictive practices was, of course, common to many industries. Price maintenance, for example, had always been present amongst local traders, and gained the support of manufacturers during the 1880s, most notably in cycles, drapery, drugs, spirits, tobacco, groceries, and confectionery. Its practitioners argued that price-cutters merely undermined the profitability of an industry and prevented the development of new, better quality products. As more and more goods became packaged and branded, and to some degree reliant upon the advertising of unique selling properties rather than price, it was an increasingly-heard argument. The maintenance of prices and profit margins also supported a network of small retailers who could provide a direct and available service to consumers. Moreover, traders would often do business only with established or accredited firms, and would seek to maintain traditional market roles in the manufacture, delivery or sale of particular goods. Such arrangements might maintain specific skills and expertise, and, like price mainten- ance, keep intact a dealer and retailing network. Restrictive practices, on the other hand, could protect inefficient firms and instill market rigidities, so keeping prices and profits 'artificially' high. But criticisms of restrictive practices were comparatively muted – the government's investigations of the issue after the War were eventually fruitless – and the maintenance of prices and established trading relationships was widely accepted.[5]

There is no doubt that the timber trade tried to protect itself from the greater competition encouraged by the economically depressed 1920s. The question of traditional trading relationships and price-cutting had not been important during the continuous expansion in the demand for wood before the Great War. But, in the following decade, they became a central issue, as suppliers resorted to exclusive selling arrangements and preferential pricing. The timber trade turned to the device of approved lists which restricted the number of competitors, sellers and buyers. It argued that unrestricted competition would have hurt reputable firms, traditional skills and knowledge, and overall standards of service. Firms contended that unlimited price-cutting, moreover, would force the industry to concentrate upon quick-selling types and sizes of timber. Critics, of course, held that prices were artificially high and, being fixed, distorted changes in the demand for timber types and sizes. To be exact, price collusion was probably rare – though firms would work within 'accepted' scales – but the approved lists did maintain a structure of agents, importers, merchants, and consumers when, perhaps, the combination of functions might have brought economies and better service.

There was another outcome to this increased tendency towards restrictive practices: firms were given an incentive to join the trade association since it settled the terms of entry to an approved list of dealers. Due to the existence of different sectors within the business, these approved lists were actually managed by the many, semi- autonomous sections which composed the Timber Trade Federation. As we have seen so many times, the TTF operated as a fissiparous organisation which combined many sections that largely conducted their own affairs but united when necessary for the sake of mutual interest.[6]

The largest timber sector – the softwood trade – became interested in restrictive agreements soon after the Great War. In 1919, the National Softwood Importers' Section of the TTF was concerned that merchants and end-users could purchase small lots of timber at dock-sale auctions directly from the shippers' agent or brokers. Much of this wood was composed of unsold portions of consignment cargoes, often included to fill space in the ship's hold, and, as a consequence, it could be bought at a low price. Sometimes, it was carried alongside orders from large importers and under separate bills of lading, and, furthermore, these lots did not carry demurrage costs at the ports. After talks with the Timber Agents' and Brokers' Association of the United Kingdom – which traded in softwood and it was itself a member of the TTF – agents agreed wherever possible to sell only to the importers described as 'legitimate' by an approved list drawn up by the NSIS. But the non-binding agreement did not prove effective, and, in 1921, the TTF's Executive Council complained to Scandinavian shippers about the levels of softwood imports handled without the intervention of importers. The shippers replied that they also dealt with some 250 'non-approved' importers, and, given conditions of over-supply in the inter-war period, they were wary of limiting the number of potential purchasers.

Insecurity in the softwood trade was widespread: prices were generally falling, and the revolutionary government in Russia accelerated this problem by 'dumping' supplies in return for much-needed foreign exchange. Negotiations followed over the composition of the approved list, despite protests from the Merchants Section of the TTF that, in fact, continued to be ignored throughout the inter-war period. Non-importing merchants could, however, take initial comfort from the failure of shippers and importers to come to terms. In June 1924, the NSIS passed a unanimous resolution that sales of all Swedish and Finnish softwoods should be made only through shippers' accredited agents in the UK and an agreed list of importing firms. The Swedish Wood Exporters' Association responded by asking its members not to negotiate with the NSIS for timber in 1924, but the Finnish Sawmill Owners' Association, most of whose trade passed through importers, pressed for some compromise. An agreement – reached in 1924 – specified the role of shipper, agent and importer, and expanded the approved list beyond membership of the NSIS, yet the exporters insisted that they would only recommend, not compel, their agents to work with recommended firms. The agreement was not formally ratified with the Swedish shippers until 1926, at a conference in Stockholm, as a result of which the Finnish accepted similar terms, but subsequent talks with Danzig and Norwegian exporters were not conclusive. The British importers still wanted the agents to deal with them alone, but no approved list would be effective without the support of shippers.[7]

Specific difficulties were created by the 'dumping' policies of the Soviet government, and some firms responded by seeking exclusive deals which maintained prices. In 1924, 16 of the largest British traders in softwood formed the British

Syndicate (Russian Softwood Importers) Ltd, which agreed to purchase all the timber sent by the Bolshevik government. The Syndicate, having monopolised the purchase of these softwoods, then organised the distribution, and fixed import and minimum resale prices. One prime mover in the group, Churchill & Sim, had already fought a court battle by which restrictions on imports from a government not then recognised by Britain were overturned. The firm also founded the Russian Wood Agency to sell Soviet exports to the British Empire. Not surprisingly, opponents of the Syndicate and other shippers criticised the deal and, of course, trade with the Bolshevik government aroused political controversy, partly in reaction to the Revolution and partly because much Russian timber may have been the product of slave labour camps. The arrangement forced Swedish and Finnish shippers to lower their prices. But, during the economic slump of 1929, the Syndicate was unable to absorb all the Russian timber available, and, with the Bolshevik government increasingly discontent with the prices it was obtaining, negotiations to renew the contract foundered in the following year.

From 1930, the Russians attempted to sell their products direct to the merchant trade. Naturally, the exclusive deal had angered traders outside the Syndicate, and, representing the majority of British importers, they established the Central Softwood Buying Corporation Ltd in its place and began to handle Russian softwood supplies in 1931. Exclusive dealing with the Russians, moreover, not only irritated sections of the British timber trade, but, in addition, the Canadian lumber industry. British Columbia was highly dependent on its wood exports to Britain and felt threatened by what it saw as 'dumping' arrangements. Its timber producers conducted throughout the 1930s a lengthy publicity campaign promoting its goods and attacking the Russian supplies, an issue which became embroiled after the imposition of a general tariff with its demand for imperial preference.[8] With regard to Swedish and Finnish softwoods, it was the great depression of the 1930s which altered the opinions of the shippers towards an approved list. The more competitive conditions were seen as a great threat to overall price levels. In particular, many of the smaller Swedish and Finnish exporters that were not members of their respective trade associations were trying to win customers by under-cutting: to avoid a free-fall in prices, the majority of shippers became interested in a restrictive arrangement. A joint Softwood Agreement Committee, containing equal numbers of agents and importers, was formed in October 1935 to create an approved list of dealers. Over two years of negotiations, the shippers and agents accepted a binding agreement to sell only to those on the importers' approved list, and the importers agreed to buy all their European softwood from those who adhered to their list. In accepting the latter condition, the importers had obtained a cut of one third in the numbers of approved firms, so leaving 583, of which 103 were not affiliated to the Timber Trade Federation. There were 84 accepted agents. The TTF undertook to advise other Baltic and European exporters of the new arrangements. Scandinavian shippers especially benefited because their agents, now linked to an approved list of importers, tended to work exclusively for them. In 1938, agents and importers in Liverpool and Manchester, which were largely responsible for softwood imports from North America, also formed an approved list.[9]

In the hardwood trade, it was the US shippers which had the determinant influence upon trading relations between firms. In 1922, the Hardwood Section of the TTF considered a detailed scheme which delineated the sphere of each trader in American hardwood and mahogany and decided which were 'legitimate' traders. But the market was of a specialist nature, and merchants and consumers often preferred to order and buy direct. There was not – as in softwood – such a pressing need for the general, all-purpose agent and importer, for hardwood was a comparatively high value product bought in smaller quantities. Consequently, the National Lumber Exporters Association of the USA – a powerful organisation in the international hardwood trade – had a tradition of selling directly, and refused to give their vital support to any approved list scheme. The economic circumstances of 1930s, however, eventually caused a change of view. As a result, the Hardwood Section of the TTF divided in 1936 in order to open negotiations between agents and importers: a Hardwood Agents and Brokers Association Ltd was formed alongside a Hardwood Importers' Section, and there was also a joint, coordinating committee. By 1939, an approved list had been drawn up, but traditional trading relationships and practices soon undermined its efficacy. In any case, the pact did not cover railway sleepers and staves, and the government, in response to the ensuing conflict, was soon to undertake the purchase of timber itself. No effective approved list operated until decontrol of the hardwood trade some years after the Second World War (*see* Chapter IV).[10]

The formation of a Plywood Section within the TTF in 1923 demonstrated the increasingly important part of plywood in the international timber trade. Agents, brokers, importers and merchants could all apply for membership. The Plywood Section first considered restrictive arrangements in 1925, and, in 1929, two sub-sections for agents and importers and a joint committee were established. These two groups signed an agreement in 1931 to end 'excessive fluctuations and uncertainties' in supplies and prices, and their 18 plywood agents and brokers decided to sell solely to the some 60 plywood importers, who, in turn, would only buy from accredited agents and brokers. But their membership was too small and the agreement did not cover Russian plywood. Within a year, the Finnish Plywood Manufacturers' Association objected that many of its agents were not on the approved list and withdrew its support. Without the cooperation of the Russians, the arrangement had been in any case impractical, and many shippers, agents and importers wanted the freedom to develop a fairly young trade. Attempts to reinstate restrictive practices failed in 1935, but, in 1937, the rules of the Plywood Section were revised and bound all members to comply with an approved list. Within a year, many shippers, including the Russians and the Finns, had agreed, and the lists operated until the outbreak of war.[11]

By the end of the 1930s, therefore, the three main sections of the timber trade were controlled through a system of approved lists. Refusal of admission effectively barred traders from dealing as shippers' agents or importers in these product types. Within the Timber Trade Federation, the activities of agents and importers in softwood, hardwood, and plywood were in each case coordinated through joint committees that would decide upon entry or refusal as a 'legitimate' trader to their particular approved list. Again, it was the agent with the support of the shipper and the larger, all-purpose importers which dominated the trade and the affairs of the TTF, their central position aided by their concentration within London. The views of non-importing merchants throughout Britain – by far the greatest number of firms – were not considered. Agents were allowed to join approved lists with proof of appointment by at least one shipper, and, in softwood and plywood, they had in addition to join the Timber Agents' and Brokers' Association or the Plywood Agents' Sub-Section of the TTF. These procedures and the influence of the shipper in particular adequately controlled the numbers and operations of agents. Indeed, restrictive practices would not have been possible without the support finally offered by softwood exporters from Sweden and Finland, Finnish plywood manufacturers, and American hardwood shippers.

Inclusion as a recognised importer was more complicated and a large degree of discretion was exercised by the various joint committees. Applicants, however, had in practice to be non-importing merchants, and, in order to limit numbers, they had to demonstrate an ability to develop a 'sound' business. In softwood, a trader had to import some 1,000 standards (approximately 4,700 cubic metres) per annum, and hardwood and plywood dealers had annually to buy goods to the value of £20,000 and £75,000 respectively. Proof that an importer actually consumed timber was considered adequate reason for refusal. There were significant sections of the industry not affected by the approved list system – especially pitwood and staves – simply because end-users such as collieries, coopers, and food and drink firms had historically obtained their supplies direct from shippers. Conversely, the agent and importer had traditional and central roles in the softwood, hardwood and plywood business, and it was the undermining of their position during the inter-war period which led finally to the formal introduction of restrictive practices.[12]

In short, fluctuations in the demand for and the price of timber after the Great War began to affect the organisation of timber supplies, and spurred international exporters and influential British firms to resist re-structuring and unrestricted competition. One other factor also had a significant impact upon the nature of demand for timber and the character of the trade. As the motor lorry began to undermine the railways' dominance of freight carriage – most notably in short-haul traffic – importers and merchants found they could deliver timber at short notice. They could, therefore, more regularly supply their customers with specifications which met their requirements and the needs of a particular job more precisely. Stock levels could, as a result, be minimised. In highly competitive circumstances, speed of delivery and the more exact matching of consumption requirements emerged as important marketing tools. Importers pressed shippers to invest more extensively in sawmilling, and so export the specifications used by consumers. Otherwise, ships would carry an uneconomical amount of unwanted and unsellable cargo. Importers themselves also had to invest in sawmilling operations if they were to meet the more immediate orders of merchants. Developments in the timber market had a dual, sometimes conflicting impact. Many importers and merchants had to deal in more types and sizes once only obtained from different traders. But, to facilitate the rapid matching of supply and demand, the overall number of specifications needed in the timber trade fell, and the product became more standardised. As we have seen, transport issues and timber were inextricably linked, simply because it was a raw material brought from all over the world to every region of the country. Shipping links, dock developments, and railways were basic questions for an internationally-traded commodity, but, in the 1920s, the greater use of the motor lorry transformed short-haul traffic and influenced the nature of the market.[13]

III: IMPERIAL PREFERENCE AND HOUSING, 1930–1938

The growing tendency to control prices and market relationships originated from the less stable demand for timber in the inter-war period and from a situation of over-supply. It is not surprising that these problems were accentuated by the economic depression of 1929–32, but political changes also had an important impact on the timber trade. In order to correct a deteriorating balance of payments and as a means of aiding British industry, the government from 1931 abandoned the Gold Standard and a general policy of free trade, and introduced protective duties. As large-scale importers, the Timber Trade Federation and its members were wary of these changes. But they did benefit from a number of favourable trends in the 1930s that were in themselves a partial consequence of changes in exchange rate and trade policy, particularly a low bank rate. The demand for timber expanded because a general fall in commodity prices and a rise in living standards combined with cheap money to stimulate a housing boom.

The Gold Standard was a nominal notion that paper currency could be directly traded for gold and that, in addition, the 'gold content' of sterling was 486 per cent that of the US dollar. Given the absence of exchange controls, there was, in theory, a freedom to convert currency into gold, and to do so at levels fixed by the 'gold content' of each currency. Then, this nominal gold could be converted into another currency, once more at some set ratio. As a consequence, exchange rates were prevented from fluctuating outside narrow bands. In fact, each country's Standard bore very little relation to the comparative value of currencies or to a nation's current account. But it had been seen as crucial to the credibility of the international monetary and trading system before the Great War, not because gold was plentiful enough to guarantee the value of all paper currency but because national central banks had cooperated to control and maintain the flow of gold and credits. In effect, increases in bank rates could attract capital and fund temporary deficits in the balance of payments, with the result that movements in exchange rates were limited and, indeed, stabilised around the Gold Standard. Britain itself was particularly aided by the availability of sterling balances throughout the Empire and in countries which bought its manufactures.

When international cooperation disappeared during the Great War, the British government adopted a floating currency in order to make adjustments to the current account, especially as the country's import needs increased and its export potential declined. To prevent capital going abroad, exchange controls were imposed, and wartime expenditure had to be partly funded through a monetary expansion which had little connection with Gold Standard theory. The British government, like many others, sought a return to the 'certainties' of the Gold Standard and fixed exchange rates after the war. It saw the old system as a key-stone to exchange rate and trade stability, and viewed the Gold Standard and a highly valued pound as a symbol of economic strength. It was assumed too that the Gold Standard, because it represented the paper currency's intrinsic value, would place limits on the money supply, as well as necessitating a high exchange rate of $4.86, in which case, it would serve as an anti-inflationary device that would make British companies more competitive. On the other hand, when the Gold Standard was finally reintroduced in 1925, a number of factors which had underpinned the system no longer existed. The cooperation between national banks had declined; many established, mutually-beneficial trading relationships had disappeared; and the need for sterling on the foreign exchanges had been depleted by Britain's loss of markets for its staple industries. Imports of timber – between 3 and 4.4 per cent of all import values in the 1920s – undoubtedly contributed to the strains on Britain's current account. The economic depression of 1929–32 delivered the final blow to established economic 'certainties': Britain was finally forced by a run on the pound and a deteriorating current account to abandon the Gold Standard and revert to a floating exchange rate.[14]

How did devaluation affect the international timber trade? There were immediate difficulties for British firms which had purchased goods in foreign currencies, and a number of Scandinavian shippers found difficulty fulfilling contracts with importers which had paid in sterling. Increases in the price of timber following devaluation proved a passing problem as supplier countries left the Gold Standard, although the Finnish showed reluctance to review exchange and monetary arrangements. It was the repercussions of Gold Standard's abandonment in other policy areas which were more influential. By not having to sustain a high exchange rate, the government could adopt a bank rate of 2 per cent. The effects of cheap money on the wider economy are disputable, but the importance of available credit for the construction industry, housing and the demand for timber was direct. The reduction in bank rate combined in the 1930s with a number of demand factors – the fall in commodity prices, the general rise in living standards, the development and growth of 'new' industries like electricals, chemicals, motor cars, and food processing – to favour the timber trade. Indeed, Anderson's of Islington became associated with the film industry. The nearby Gainsborough Film Studio required large amounts of timber during its construction, but it continued to demand plywood and other materials for its sets. Brownlee & Company of Glasgow experienced rising orders from cabinet-makers, furniture craftsmen and office-fitters.[15]

Alongside the ending of the Gold Standard, another part of the old trading system was abandoned. The British government hoped that a lower and floating exchange rate might correct a negative balance of payments. It, likewise, recanted free trade in the expectation that tariffs too could restrict import levels. The election of the National Government in October placed the pro-protection majority in the Conservative Party in an influential position, and some response to the raising of tariff barriers throughout the world was required. Britain had historically placed revenue-raising duties on certain commodities, and in the case of sugar they tended to protect the indigenous beet industry. Other tariffs on luxury items were implemented during the First World War to save on foreign exchange, and many of these had been retained. Later legislation designed to safeguard strategic and key industries – like dyestuffs, scientific instruments, and cars – and also to prevent dumping had had a wider effect. But Britain remained, on the whole, attached to a policy of international free trade until 1932, when some temporary tariffs were imposed.

Under the Import Duties Act, passed early in 1932, a 10 per cent *ad valorem* duty was placed on goods entering the country, although Empire products, those already protected, foodstuffs and essential industrial raw materials were excepted for the time being. This temporary arrangement did, however, affect most timber imports, the only exceptions being hewn but not sawn or planed timber and wooden pitprops. It was acknowledged that Britain could not replace the timber it obtained in the main from the Baltic, but the government was anxious to encourage indigenous sawmilling operations. Pitprops were designated as a vital industrial raw material. In the longer term, the government was considering the question of imperial preference, in which Britain would import food and raw materials from the Empire free of duty or at special rates, and the dominions and colonies would receive manufactured goods from Britain on similar terms, the aim being to create a worldwide economic bloc. With regard to the trade in timber, the chief issue was whether exports from British Columbia could substitute softwoods and hardwoods from non-Empire areas. An Imports Duties Advisory Committee was appointed to advise on all aspects of future tariff policy. It had to consider all goods subject to the temporary general tariff, and, taking into account the interests of consuming and producing industries, decide whether such products might be made in Britain. Under the Act, therefore, imports could be placed on a Free List.[16]

Representing an industry reliant upon one of Britain's largest imports, the Timber Trade Federation argued that, whilst imperial preference was being considered, wood should be imported free of tariffs. Duties might harm the timber trade, and, before they were imposed, the TTF first wanted arrangements with countries like Canada which could replace any reliance on the Baltic. Indeed, the Federation offered its support for imperial preference. It additionally sought restrictions on planed, moulded and semi-manufactured products, in the hope of encouraging home manufacture. But it was strongly opposed to duties being imposed on sawn softwood planks, deals, battens and boards, the largest item in the timber trade. Exporters had increasingly taken on sawmilling operations, partly to save on shipping space but partly also in response to customers' very wishes. Before its arrival at a British port, wood was cut to size, and often planed and moulded. As the country did not have the industrial capacity to saw all its timber imports, the TTF argued that tariffs on sawn softwoods were merely increasing costs without the prospect of compensating advantages. It depicted these duties as punitive, unfair taxation-raising measures rather than as a device for protecting British economic interests. The home-grown timber trade, of course, took a contrary view. Interestingly, France at the time placed limitations on imports in the hope of encouraging indigenous forestry. In Britain, the most important issue and the primary cause of dispute was the future of the Baltic softwood trade. The trade feared that higher costs for consumers would further diminish the demand for timber, and make it more difficult for Scandinavian producers to maintain price levels. Oversupply, as we have noted, threatened the structure of the timber trade, and, by the 1930s, was even converting shippers to the cause of approved lists and restrictive practices. In preparing for negotiations with the Imports Duties Advisory Committee, the various sections within the TTF formed sub-committees, but the Federation was able to achieve a consensus over different products. The Softwood Tariff Sub-Committee agreed with duties varying between 15 and 50 per cent for items such as doors, mouldings, skirtings, boxes, and box parts, but, not surprisingly, argued the case that other types of sawn products should enter free. The Hardwood Tariff Sub-Committee urged that it would generally prove uneconomic to cut the smaller amounts of imported hardwood in Britain, although there was a case for imperial preference being given to mahogany supplies. Its plywood counterpart saw no point in tariffs when the country was reliant on foreign supplies and sawmilling, and it was backed by toy, furniture, perambulator and invalid carriage makers.[17]

The Imports Duties Advisory Committee finally reported in April 1932, and, as a result, tariffs of 15 per cent were placed on builders' wood such as window-frames, doors and gates, while other manufactured items with the exception of machinery-parts, tools, and medical apparatus were subjected to a 20 per cent rate. The 10 per rate on non-manufactured softwood, hardwood and plywood products remained. The Imperial Economic Conference, held in Ottawa that year to discuss issues of imperial preference, was of direct relevance to the timber trade, and governments and businessmen convened to discuss the possibility of a trading bloc. The TTF formed part of the Federation of British Industry's delegation. The mercantilist image of an industrial mother country dealing with primary producer colonies, however, was anachronistic, because industries existed throughout the Empire, Britain was determined to protect its own agricultural interests, and trade with foreign countries was generally too important. The Conference achieved only a series of bilateral agreements in which a system of quotas and licences sought to encourage trade within the Empire.

In talks over the timber trade between Canada and Britain, the negotiations were complicated by a number of factors. Logging was central to the economic life of British Columbia, but the province had over decades lost its British markets to Baltic and other producers. By the early 1930s, the USA was increasingly closing its borders, and Japan – at one time absorbing some 40 per cent of output from British Columbia – was developing imperial interests in Manchuria and obtaining ever greater supplies from Siberia. Concessions from Britain were, therefore, vital. Although the Canadians were granted a 10 per cent preference for five years, they believed any consequent advantage to be lost while the Russians continued to 'dump' timber in Britain. But the TTF – many of whose members benefited from the low price of Soviet wood – resisted all attempts to impose quotas. The Canadian High Commission in London and exporters continued to lobby the British government and public opinion throughout the 1930s in a somewhat heated campaign. But, by 1938, 48 per cent of all lumber cut in British Columbia went to Britain; the percentage of timber imports originating from Canada rose from 5.2 in 1929 to 16 in 1938. Furthermore, the existence of tariffs did give the British government enough leverage to conduct throughout the decade a series of bilateral agreements similar to those reached at the Ottawa conference. The unfavourable trade balances with the Baltic countries, to which timber imports contributed to no small degree, were corrected by agreements to buy more British exports such as coal.[18] Such arrangements helped minimise the impact which timber imports continued to have on Britain's balance of trade, and the fall in commodity prices – including those of timber – on the whole favoured large importers like Britain. But the country had, with the single exception of 1935, a negative balance of payments between 1931 and 1938.[19]

What effect, then, did the housing boom have? The construction industry had undoubtedly been stimulated since the Great War by a succession of Housing Acts. Government subsidies under legislation in 1919 led to local authorities and private enterprise constructing 155,000 and 44,000 houses respectively. Commercial builders also built another 54,000 without subsidy. The 1919 Act was replaced by others in 1923 and 1924, and these by 1930 accounted for 358,000 local authority houses and 378,000 subsidised dwellings. Private enterprise was solely responsible for a further 536,000 between 1923 and 1930, and another 200,000 houses were begun by local authorities under the Acts between 1930 and 1933. The Timber Trade Federation was involved in a minor way in the planning of this legislation, and gave assurances that timber was plentiful enough to fulfil its objectives. The Housing Act of 1930 accounted for only 289,000 local authority homes and 8,000 by private enterprise. The housing boom of the 1930s, which led to the construction of some 3m homes, occurred, therefore, almost entirely in the commercial sector. These dwellings largely supplied a middle-class market, and the shortage of cheap accommodation remained as acute as ever. Clearly, trends in commodity prices, increased living standards for those who were employed, the expansion of 'new' industries, and mild recovery amongst 'old', staple concerns – rather than government intervention – accounted for any favourable trends. Given the pulling down or clearing of 700,000 dwellings between 1920–38, net total stock rose from 9.25m to 12.5m, and over two-thirds of this increase can be attributed to developments in the 1930s.[20] In 1932, 218,000 houses were built in Britain; in 1937, 362,000, a 66 per cent increase. The fall in the cost of building materials – it fell faster than the general price level – directly aided the boom in housing starts. The sharp decline in the price of Swedish timber in the early 1930s was particularly beneficial, although rises began again in 1936. It is no surprise, therefore, that the volume of timber imports rose by some 32 per cent between 1932 and 1937.[21]

In summary, the 1930s witnessed economic circumstances which were encouraging for the timber industry, yet the TTF became concerned about the growing use of substitute construction materials – principally steel and concrete – and 700 firms or 47 per cent of its membership founded the Timber Development Association Limited in March 1934. The issue of substitutes and the uses of timber had been discussed by a special committee at the TTF for a decade, but there now was support amongst British firms for a new organisation which could promote the commodity. The new body was anxious to win the active backing of overseas shippers, who were keen to protect their markets. At the 1936 Ideal Home Exhibition at Olympia and at the Empire Exhibition in 1938, the TDA tried to promote wooden houses and buildings. These marketing ideas had little appeal in Britain's climatic conditions, and the impact of the TDA was limited during the 1930s. In any case, the demand for timber was expanding, despite the greater use of substitutes, and the trade did not feel inclined to commit large resources to research.[22] Then, the development of the market for timber became secondary to the return of other issues: with the prospect of another war, controls on imports and consumption emerged as the paramount problem. Once more, the supply of timber would have to be conserved.

V: WAR-TIME CONTROLS, 1939–1945

After the Munich crisis of 1938, when Britain and France overlooked their guarantees of Czechoslovakia's security, it was clear to the National Government that it might soon be involved in further conflict with Germany. The agreement with Hitler did provide Britain with some time to prepare defences, and the government began to take questions of economic planning for war seriously. The state, therefore, started to consult and cooperate with representative trade associations like the Timber Trade Federation. The TTF entered discussions on the availability of supplies, price stability, and, ironically, given the history of the Second World War, the use of timber in trench construction. The President of the Federation and a director of Louis Bamberger & Sons, Major Archibald Harris, was nominated 'Shadow Timber Controller' and instructed to recruit a 'shadow staff'. The TTF also designed a scheme which established Advisory Committees of the various sections able to assist any future Controller, and skeleton price lists of various types of wood and grades were drawn up, to be enforced whenever necessary. The Federation coordinated, too, with the Ministry of Supply when it was established in 1939. This new department was given powers to accrue stocks of strategic materials, including timber. The storage requirements of war stimulated a demand for prefabricated buildings, so by historical accident, the work of the Timber Development Association finally proved useful: its standardised designs for wooden huts and buildings were accepted by the War Office.[23]

When war was declared in September 1939, the lessons of economic planning – acquired during the previous conflict – were soon applied. The Forestry Commission was divided into two sections: the Forest Management Department and the Timber Production Department were created to maximise the supply and processing of home-grown wood. As in the Great War, the state would have to enlarge the indigenous timber industry, and found a network of saw-mills and workshops which could operate to War Office specifications. At the Ministry of Supply, the Timber Control Department was immediately established with Archibald Harris now as official Controller. All government departments were expanded and new ministries were founded to prosecute the war effectively, and staff involved with economic planning had to be drawn from various trades and industries. The Timber Control staff, located at Bristol and in regional offices, were likewise recruited from the TTF and member firms. In order to improve cooperation and coordination with the industry, the Ministry of Supply agreed to an Advisory Committee, chaired by Leonard Arnott, which could liaise with the trade's many sections. To effect control over imports, prices, purchases, and consumption, five orders were issued during the first month of the war. The services of established agents and brokers were used to obtain supplies from abroad under a scheme of state purchase. Only pitprops for South Wales collieries remained outside control measures, but they finally came under the

Ministry's aegis some 18 months later. The Timber Control took possession of all landed softwoods – the bulk of imports – at an early stage and later directly handled hardwood and plywood. All resales and consumption were strictly controlled according to a quota system and once military requirements had been met.[24] As a result, the level of timber imports was constrained (Table II).

TABLE II

Imports of Timber into the UK, in Current and Constant Values (£) and Quantities, 1939–1945

Year	Current Value £	Wholesale Price Index	Constant Value £	Cubic m millions
1939	39.8	79.4	50.1	10.3
1940	40.5	145.6	27.8	5.7
1941	26.7	189.2	14.1	3.2
1942	22.1	224.6	9.8	2.4
1943	38.3	288.7	13.3	3.3
1944	43.6	332.4	13.1	3.5
1945	52.7	319.9	16.5	5.1

Source: Appendix III.

Moreover, timber was increasingly put to military uses by the Admiralty, Ministry of Supply, the War Office, the Ministry of Aircraft Production, and the Air Ministry (Table III).

TABLE III

Consumption of Timber, 1941–45

Softwoods: (1000s tons)	1941	1942	1943	1944	1945
Total munitions	1260.0	1309.9	1325.3	1662.1	1430.6
Non-munitions	641.5	515.1	492.4	604.3	898.1
Grand Total	1901.1	1825.0	1817.6	2266.4	2328.7
Hardwoods: (cu ft m):	1941	1942	1943	1944	1945
Total munitions	49.0	65.6	70.5	67.0	58.7
Non-munitions	46.7	47.7	61.1	57.8	71.4
Grand total	95.7	113.3	131.6	124.8	130.1

Source: Board of Trade; Hurstfield, p.451.

Because of timber's strategic importance and Britain's reliance upon imports, controls were immediately imposed on timber, as they were on steel, metals, cotton, fibres, rubber, sugar, fuel and petrol in 1939. The level of intervention in the timber trade was by no means matched by the action taken in the majority of other industries. The government recognised the need to mobilise the whole economy behind the war-effort, but was distracted by other priorities. Its first task was to equip the British Expeditionary Force sent to Europe, and there was no immediate threat to the nation's safety or control of the seas and shipping routes. There was no emergency in the overall supply position until the fall of Denmark and Norway in April 1940 and defeat of France during the following May. Softwood imports from the Baltic – some 70 per cent of softwood totals before the war – could not be obtained, and, with German troops across the English Channel, all British shipping routes were endangered. Small quantities from Russia could be purchased, but Canada had in future to supply some four-fifths of softwood requirements. The Canadians, therefore, practically monopolised the British market during the Second World War, the increase in the Atlantic trade during the previous decade proving an unpredicted and quickly-exploited boon.[25]

Most of the controls for timber were already being operated by 1940, but the creation of a Timber Control Board in May was in part a response to the new emergency. There was a re-invigorated drive to reduce dependency on imports. Much timber was saved from bombed buildings, and packing materials were recycled. Nevertheless, there was one main difficulty: home production was hindered by the shortage of manpower. But labour was soon brought from Canada, Australia and New Zealand and members of the Women Timber Corps were recruited. As a result, 5,793 acres were felled during 1940 – compared to the annual pre-war average of 622 – and the Forestry Commission achieved an enhanced average 4,360 acres during the six war years. Most of the timber required for small naval craft, warplanes, and collieries was eventually found from indigenous sources.[26] The widespread demand on labour and withdrawals to other industries, however, led to a decline in the numbers employed in 1942, and the Sawmilling and Woodworking Section of the TTF was concerned that the Forestry Commission would establish its own, directly-managed production units. It persuaded the government that it could cope with the supply of timber and that the Commission should found its own mills only in inaccessible areas. During 1943, recruitment problems had been overcome, and the indigenous timber industry reached its maximum strength. Indeed, the Timber Control Board – formed during a time of urgency and emergency to coordinate the efforts of the home-grown and import trade – was seen as having achieved its task and was disbanded. The Forestry Commission, working with the Home Timber Production Department at the Ministry of Supply, and the Timber Control began to administer their respective tasks separately. Wartime needs had in general been met, but at a significant cost: by 1945, 60 per cent of the nation's softwoods and 40 per cent of its hardwoods had been felled.[27]

The changing position of imports and home-grown timber is reflected in the figures.

During 1940–44, indigenous woods had to replace foreign sources, and imports did not regain their primary importance until 1945 (Table IV).

TABLE IV

Imports and Home Production of Timber, 1942–1945 (1000s tons)

Home Production:	1942	1943	1944	1945
Softwoods	745	720	490	325
Hardwoods	920	1129	1044	915
Pitwood	1529	1901	1506	1260
Total	3257	2029	3040	2500
Imports	**1942**	**1943**	**1944**	**1945**
Softwoods	781	1349	1137	1891
Hardwoods	271	275	360	360
Pitwood	28	71	186	484
Total:	1080	1695	1683	2735

Source: Board of Trade; Hurstfield, p.473.

After the entry of the USA into the war in 1941 and the victories at El Alamein and Stalingrad in 1942, Churchill's coalition government began to consider issues of post-war reconstruction. The extreme threat to Britain's security had passed, and, for the sake of national morale, some outline of a better future after the conflict had to be planned and promoted. During the last years of the Second World War, questions of medical treatment, sick pay, pensions, education, and employment were the focus of reconstruction proposals. The government, in direct or indirect control of most industries, had to consider the ownership and structure of the peace-time economy and the future interests of consumers, and a Ministry of Reconstruction was established in 1943. There was, however, no possibility of relaxing economic controls: for example, the USA was consuming nearly all the timber it was producing, and the German submarine threat to shipping remained.

The timber trade was involved with two aspects of reconstruction proposals. The Forestry Commission and the Home Grown Production Department in 1943 published a report on forestry policy after the war, an important issue considering the rate of depletion at the time. It suggested that the Commission should acquire 2m acres of woodland and a further 3m for planting, and the Forestry Act of 1945 provided the Commission with the necessary authority to achieve these objectives. The other major issue, housing, was central to future health and welfare policy. Therefore, Bryan Latham, the TTF's Vice-President, was appointed official representative on the Directorate of Post-War Building, formed by the Ministry of

Works and Planning. To ensure the fullest use of timber on the return to peace, the links between the TTF and the Timber Development Association were strengthened. It was agreed that the Federation's Vice-President would automatically become the TDA's President, and that the TTF would nominate 22 of the Association's 30 Council members. Decontrol issues and the re-establishment of the Baltic markets also formed the subject of policy discussions between the TTF, the Timber Control Department and the Ministry of Supply.[28]

The Federation had operated during the war as a liaison between government and the timber trade, and had had a role in the prosecution of the war-effort and the saving of valuable shipping space, foreign currency, and unnecessary consumption. The TTF was consulted on issues of quotas, remuneration, pool arrangements, and war risk insurance. It was particularly anxious that the Timber Control should use established firms, and prevent consumers obtaining their requirements directly. As Leonard Arnott, the TTF's President, declared in 1942: 'if the Federation had not succeeded in preserving the structure of the Trade intact it had done much to prevent it being completely destroyed.' Having established approved lists before the war to maintain traditional trading arrangements, the TTF was anxious that post-war circumstances did not lead to major re-structuring. On other hand, the TTF could not easily enforce decisions upon its members. Within the Federation, schemes to centralise decision-making between 1940–3 failed, despite the fact that a well-organised TTF would have had greater influence upon the government and, by helping to administer controls, it would have been better placed to preserve the trade's structure. Although the expertise of Federation officers and members was brought into the Ministry of Supply at the outbreak of war, the TTF itself acted largely as an adviser, and the state through the Ministry and the Forestry Commission actually operated the controls. As an essential, imported resource requiring a high proportion of shipping space, timber was naturally the object of immediate intervention and so remained under direct supervision. The example of confectionery manufacture, where the industry itself operated the controls, was far from typical.[29]

VI: DE-CONTROL, 1945–1952

The recently-elected Labour government was aware that Britain had fought the war by consuming capital and turning industries over to military purposes, and that the termination of lend-lease arrangements by the USA would leave the country unable to pay for essential imports. The arrival of peace had brought a balance of payments and sterling crisis. The government was forced to negotiate a loan from the USA, and in return it agreed to lift all forms of tariffs and Empire preference. Without protective duties, Britain had to retain economic controls and rationing schemes, because levels of import and consumption had to be minimised and exports had to be encouraged and maximised. It was estimated that the volume of exports would have to be increased by at least 75 per cent to redress the balance of trade, pay off the sterling debt, and build up gold and dollar reserves. The ending of the conflict had, in short, an ironic consequence: as economic difficulties gave place to economic crisis, government controls had to be extended. Austerity worsened after 1945, and fuel shortages during the winter of 1946–7 were acute. To prevent the collapse of Western Europe and the spread of Communism, the USA decided to offer its allies Marshall Aid in 1948. This help coincided with the Labour government's export drive, finally bringing a balance of payments equilibrium. Although many controls were lifted in the November of 1948, many others remained, and Britain was not able to refuse Marshall Aid until 1950. Furthermore, the tightening of controls between 1948–50 directly affected the building industry and the demand for timber, and import and consumption controls continued to block any return to a free market. Devaluation in 1949 added to the problems faced by major importers, and timber shortages allowed concrete manufacturers to expand the scope of substitutes.[30]

The government soon recognised after the war that wood would remain a scarce resource, and that state purchase, import quotas, price control and consumption licencing would have to continue. Nonetheless, the Timber Trade Federation was anxious to end controls as soon as possible and created a Decontrol Committee to negotiate with Harris, the official Controller. The government hoped to direct softwood supplies into transport, mining, shipbuilding, export industries, and housing. According to an order issued in February 1946, therefore, the Timber Control Department would continue to hold the landed stock and distribute it under licence.[31] But the softwood importers were the first to win a partial lifting of controls, and they were allowed to buy allotted quotas of supplies from nominated countries. Restrictions on the total imported remained. In order to obtain foreign timber, importers had to purchase extensively from the National Stock, and the distribution of these stored supplies became the task of a privately-funded organisation created for the purpose, the National Softwood Brokers Ltd. By allowing some private imports while setting global limits, the government was attempting to compromise between two issues: the balance-of-payments position and an unmet need for a basic material. There was a worldwide shortage of timber, partly because of war-time devastation on the Continent and partly because suppliers themselves wanted all available stocks. The Timber Control was in 1946 only able to purchase some 1.8m tons or about 32 per cent of pre-war imports (1934–8 average). Between 1946 and 1951, softwood imports amounted to approximately half of pre-war totals, and, with traditional supplies unavailable, a third of all timber was arriving from Canada.[32] Key controls on the purchase, importation, pricing and consumption of softwood – and, indeed, other types of timber – remained until the early 1950s.

There were two major reasons for this policy. For the sake of its balance-of-payments position, Britain had to limit imports, and, in a period when all raw materials were in short supply, the state had to secure supplies and determine priorities. The country, for one, was not in a position to export large amount of coal, and its ability to exchange these goods for timber from old trading partners like Sweden and Finland was limited (226,000 and 468,000 tons respectively in 1946). The Soviet Union could only send miniscule amounts (some 29,000 tons). Attempts to obtain wood from Germany as reparation payments were no long term or sufficient answer, and heavy felling had to be continued in Britain.[33] The timber supply position did dramatically improve in 1947, but worsened thereafter. The softwood supply, therefore, was not substantially eased until 1951, when demand was so great that the inflationary pressures were evident (Table V).

TABLE V

Value and Quantities of Timber Imports into the UK, 1946–1951

Year	Current Value £m	Wholesale Price Index	Constant Value (1946 = 100)	Cubic m millions
1946	62.0	319.2	62.0	5.2
1947	125.8	392.6	76.3	9.1
1948	101.8	470.8	91.4	7.1
1949	109.1	480.7	93.2	7.6
1950	101.4	507.5	98.4	6.8
1951	237.5	655.3	127.3	10.9

Source: Appendix III.

The major casualty of consequent timber and other shortages was housing. As a result of building restrictions and enemy action, it was estimated after the war that the housing shortage amounted to 1.25m dwellings. As the number of households was rising and inadequate homes had to be replaced, it was assumed that 3m new units would have to be built. Only 55,000 permanent dwellings were built in 1946; 140,000 in 1947; and some 200,000 a year in 1948–50. The government also subsidised the construction of 148,000 pre-fabricated houses. These amounted to about 800,000 dwellings in total.[34] Pitwood was required for the reconstruction of the coalmining industry: an essential fuel and the national export drive had to be maintained. The Labour government could not, therefore, consider its decontrol, and supplies continued to be directed. On nationalisation of the coalmining industry, responsibility for pitwood was shared by the Ministry of Fuel and Power and the National Coal Board. After the war the government needed to invest in Britain's run-down collieries, and pitwood remained a large, priority item in the timber trade.[35]

Private imports of certain hardwoods were allowed in 1946. But, as in the case of softwood, worldwide shortages and Britain's balance of payments difficulties prevented any major relaxation of restrictions for several years. It was not until November 1949 that the Board of Trade and the Timber Controller opened discussions with hardwood agents and importers and issued a report recommending

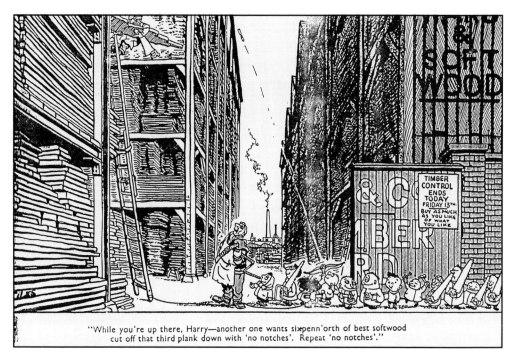

Giles Cartoon, *Sunday Express*, 15th November 1953.
Reproduced by permission of the *Sunday Express*.

full decontrol. As a result, the consumption licencing of hardwood – excepting US and Canadian exports – was lifted in the following December. The government limited dollar purchases because of their particularly direct impact on Britain's balance of payments and its ability to repay international debts. With the technical assistance of the Timber Development Association, firms responded by successfully developing the trade in colonial hardwoods. Although import restrictions and maximum prices were abolished in January 1950, an annual quota of £3m on North American hardwoods remained until 1955.[36]

Imports of plywood were heavily restricted throughout the 1940s, and only in 1950 was limited private buying allowed. State purchase continued in 'hard' currency countries that included the main sources of supply, namely Finland and the Soviet Union, as well as the United States and Canada. In order to minimise the impact of sterling purchases, consumption licencing and price control were similarly lifted only on a partial basis in 1950 and 1951 respectively. From 1952, import controls and other restrictions were ended, but all overseas contracts had to be matched by purchases from the national stock. It was not until 1955 that the plywood trade was generally freed, limits on supplies made from US hardwoods being retained until 1957.

As we have seen, the government only partly decontrolled softwood in the immediate post-war years, and, because of the size and importance of this trade, agents and importers were not free to buy from any source until the beginning of 1951. Even so, global limits and quotas for individual firms were retained. Price control was ended in March 1951, but consumer licencing continued until November 1953. The National Softwood Brokers Ltd – from which all importers had to buy – was wound up in the same year.[37]

Because of the continuation of state restrictions, the Timber Control Department remained until 1952, when its remaining duties were transferred to the Board of Trade. By that year, the majority of controls on timber had been lifted, and, as a consequence, the TTF resumed its contacts with shippers. Its first task was to renegotiate the charter parties covering the Baltic, Russia, the Pacific Coast, and Central Europe. By 1955, timber was Britain's most expensive import, worth some £192.8m or 17.2 per cent of the total bill.[38] The Federation was finally granted its main policy objective in the immediate post-war years – the decontrol of the commerce in timber – yet it wanted, too, to re-establish the trade in its pre-war structure. During the conflict and the period of economic controls, however, government became interested in the question of monopolistic practices. As in the aftermath of the previous war, the state wanted to decontrol the economy in a way that would benefit consumers and not just business. It was particularly wary of the cooperative relations established through war-time necessity between one-time rivals, and reconstruction proposals included a review of monopolistic practices. It followed, therefore, that the very market structure and organisation of the timber trade would become the focus of public scrutiny in the 1950s, and the results of these investigations had a major effect upon the industry.

REFERENCES

1. H.J. Dyos & D.H. Aldcroft, *British Transport: An Economic Survey From the 17th Century to the 20th*, 1969, pp.299–303, 342–5; M. Bowley, *The British Building Industry*, 1966, pp.36–82.

2. C.J. Savage, *An Economic History of Transport*, 1959, pp.99–100; Modern Records Centre, Federation of British Industries, Committee Files, MSS 200/F/1/1193; TTF, *Annual Report for 1921*, pp.81–5; *Annual Report for 1922*, pp.21–33; TTF, *Annual Report for 1927*, pp.36, 40.

3. Savage, 1959, pp.99–100, 132–46; Dyos & Aldcroft, pp.299–303, 308, 314–19.

4. Latham, 1965, p.79.

5. B.S. Yamey, *The Economics of Resale Price Maintenance*, 1954, pp.3–130, 133–77; *Report of Commission on Resale Price Maintenance*, 1949 (Cmd.7676) p.1.

6. Monopolies and Restrictive Practices Commission, *Report on the Supply of Imported Timber*, 1953, pp.1–8, 15–17, 20–1, 38–42; TTF, *Annual Report for 1927*, pp.73–4, 81–2; *Annual Report for 1929*, p.7.

7. *Report . . .*, 1953, pp.20–36.

8. Latham, 1965, pp.79–94, 103–4; Carvel, *One Hundred Years in Timber*, 1949, chapter 6.

9. *Report . . .*, 1953, pp.26–8, 36–9, 46–57; TTF, *Annual Report for 1932*, pp.9, 33.

10. *Report . . .*, 1953, pp.16, 22–3.

11. Ibid., pp.22–3, 26–8, 40–3; TTF, *Annual Report for 1932*, p.40.

12. Ibid., pp.2–3, 10–11, 26–8.

13. Ibid., pp.66–71.

14. Cf. I.M. Drummond, *The Gold Standard and the International Monetary System, 1900–1939*, 1987; S. Howson, *Domestic Monetary Management in Britain, 1919–38*, 1975; D.E. Moggridge, *British Monetary Policy 1924–1931*, 1972.

15. Cf. Howson, 1975; Moggridge, 1972; B.W.E. Alford, *Depression and Recovery? Economic Growth, 1918–39*, 1972; E.T. Nevin, *The Mechanism of Cheap Money: a Study of British Monetary Policy, 1931–39*, 1955; H.W. Richardson, *Economic Recovery in Britain*, 1967; A. Muir, *Anderson's of Islington: the History of C.F. Anderson & Son, Ltd., 1863–1988*, 1988, pp.20–21; Carvel, 1949, p.69.

16. Cf. I.M. Drummond, *Imperial Economic Policy*, 1974; Howson, 1975; *Annual Report for 1932*, pp.25–39, 58; *Timber Trades Journal*, 3 Oct 1931, p.2.

17. Latham, 1965, p.94; *Timber Trades Journal*, 4 April 1931, p.9; 11 July 1931, pp.78–9; 12 Sept 1931, p.704; 26 Sept 1931, p.845 13 Feb 1932, p.498; 20 Feb 1931, p.398; 21 April 1932, p.489.

18. J. Hurstfield, 'The Control of Raw Material Supplies, 1919–39', *Ec.H.R.*, 1944, pp.1–31; *Annual Report for 1932*, p.26; G.W. Taylor, *Timber: a History of the Forest Industry in British Columbia*, 1975, pp.117–23; *Timber Trades Journal*, 30 July 1932, p.184; 3 Dec 1932, p.367.

19. Mitchell, 1990, pp.453–4.

20. Latham, 1965, pp.97–8, 102; Pollard, pp.254–61.

21. Mitchell, 1990, pp. 476–7; A.P. Becker, 'Housing in England and Wales during the Business Depression of the 1930s', *Ec.H.R.*, 1950–1, p.332.

22. Hurstfield, 1944, p.25; B. Latham, 'The Story of the T.D.A. and T.R.A.D.A., 1934–74'; TTF, *Annual Report for 1934*, pp.3, 21–22, 117; TDA, *Annual Report*, 1936, p.157.

23. Hurstfield, *The Control of Raw Materials*, p. 154; Latham, 1965, p.109; *Who Was Who, 1971– · 80*, p.25; TTF, *Annual Report for 1939*, pp.9, 26, 127; Executive Council, 1 Sept 1939.

24. James, pp.226–7; G. Ryle, *English Forestry*, 1965, pp.74–5; M.M. Postan, *British War Production*, 1952, pp.295–316. From Feb 1941, the Home Timber Production Department moved from the Forestry Commission to the Ministry of Supply.

25. Taylor, 1975, pp.150–1; Pollard, pp.402–4; Latham, 1959, p.68; F. House, *Timber at War: An Account of the Organisation of the Timber Control, 1939–45*, 1965, passim.

26. Hurstfield, p.317; Pollard, p.318; Ryle, pp.74–5, 80; James, pp.229–232. At its peak, the Women's Timber Corps numbered 6,200. It was disbanded in 1946.

27. James, p.229–32.

28. Pollard, pp.356–364; Timber Development Association, *T.D.A.'s View on Timber Supplies and the Housing Programme*, 1947; James, pp.233–6; Ryle, p.104; Latham 1965, pp.121–7.

29. Latham, 1965, pp.121–7; TTF, Executive Council Minutes, 26 Jan 1944. Cf. also R. Fitzgerald, *Rowntree's and the Marketing Revolution 1897–1969*, (forthcoming).

30. Cf., e.g., Pollard, 1962, passim.

31. *Timber Trades Journal*, 5 Jan 1946, pp.39–40; Latham, 1959, p.70.

32. Latham, 1957, pp.72–92.

33. Ibid.

34. Cf. Pollard, 1962, passim.

35. Latham, 1957, p.72–92; N.Rosenberg, *Economic Planning in the British Building Industry, 1945–49*, 1960, pp.31–67, 135–51; TTF, Executive Council, 11 June 1947.

36. Latham, 1959, p.72; *Report . . .*, 1953, pp.17–18; TTF, Executive Council, 11 June 1947.

37. *Report . . .*, 1953, pp.17–18.

38. Latham, 1957, passim; Latham, 1965, passim.

─IV─
RESTRICTIVE PRACTICES AND INDUSTRIAL STRUCTURE, 1953–1972

I: THE LIBERALISATION OF TRADE

Although the government sought after 1945 to end war-time economic controls, the restrictions were lifted more gradually than had been anticipated because of continued shortages and Britain's balance of payments difficulties. But the severe economic problems faced – particularly in the years 1945–8 – did not influence domestic economic policy alone. The USA linked economic assistance after the war to its determination that tariff barriers, import quotas and exchange controls be removed. In effect, its vital aid forced compliance amongst the many countries devastated by conflict, and the *Pax Americana* emerged in the post-war years as the lynchpin of a world trading system. After all, the USA – least hurt of the combatants – was well placed to benefit from an open system of world trade. When negotiating the Mutual Aid Programme with Britain during the Second World War, the USA forced Britain to accept the principles of free trade. It was hostile to preferential arrangements within the British Empire, which it saw as imperialistic and as a particular danger to their growing export trade, and Japan's exclusion from trading blocs and the imposition of embargoes were chief motives for the attack on Pearl Harbour. It would be fair to mention, on the other hand, that the USA itself had before its commitment to free trade a long history of protectionism, particularly in the 50 or so years before the Second World War. The very strength of the dollar underpinned the fixed exchange arrangements that were agreed at Bretton Woods in 1944, the aim being to encourage the stability integral to an open trading system. Currencies were linked to gold or their US equivalent, and balance of payments difficulties could be funded through the newly-established International Monetary Fund, although devaluation was accepted whenever imbalances proved severe and long term.

But the USA's policies faced immediate problems of implementation in the post-war world. The Americans had initially to accept that many economies – including those of Western Europe – could not openly compete and allow the free movement of goods and currency. When, for example, granting to Britain the credits so badly needed after the war, they tried to enforce compliance with free trade principles. It was soon apparent that Britain was economically too weak to allow unlimited imports and the free exchange of sterling for dollars, and, following a run on the pound, the USA agreed to relax the conditions it had set. Few countries after the war could earn enough dollars to make real any commitment to free trade, and the Americans acknowledged, too, that economic reconstruction in Western Europe would depend upon Marshall Aid.[1]

In any case, Congress – more protectionist than President Truman's administration – rejected the free trade proposals formulated at the United Nations by the International Trade Organisation in 1948. A system that could take account of varying economic circumstances and interests of each country was required, and, as a result, the ITO's position was quickly undermined. At a meeting in Geneva, 23 countries simultaneously signed 123 bilateral treaties under the General Agreement on Tariffs and Trade. Import restrictions were lifted where mutually beneficial and whenever possible, and there was a clear commitment to increase the number of goods freely sold and the number of signatory countries. By 1952, there were 34 contracting nations, and their agreements covered some 80 per cent of world commerce. Although its participants agreed not to implement further preferential trade barriers, certain developments did breach the GATT arrangements: the establishment of the European Economic Community in 1957 and the European Free Trade Area in 1960 were in many aspects contrary to their spirit. Tariff reductions within EFTA would naturally harm non-participating exporters like the timber producers of British Columbia. The TTF, indeed, was worried that lower duties on manufactures would harm the domestic sawmilling of European softwood, and initially opposed membership. On the other hand, many other countries, including the USA, also continued to operate tariffs. But, generally, major reductions in import restrictions were achieved in the two decades after 1952, and, excepting agricultural products, the Kennedy Round between the USA and Europe in 1962 obtained a number of notable successes.

Indeed, rapid economic growth in many industrialised countries, the arrival of mass consumption, the demand for industrial products and raw materials, and the new international arrangements all spurred the increase in international trade. World exports amounted to US$78bn in 1953, and $574bn in 1973. Although these figures do not account for inflation, they do not incorporate the gains made in costs and efficiency either. Many economists argued that the rates of growth and material well-being achieved in the 1950s and 1960s were a direct outcome of an acceleration in world trade. It is, as usual, difficult to distinguish between domestic and international circumstances as cause or effect, yet there is less doubt that, as according to the Heckscher-Ohlin theory, countries did gain comparative and scale advantages by specialising in particular products and then exchanging these for those they did not make or possess.[2]

As Britain, therefore, lifted war-time controls, significant and contemporaneous changes in the world trading system occurred. With the coaxing of the Americans, the revocation of policies which had dominated world commerce in the years before the war was almost total: protectionism and, in some cases, a commitment to autarchy slowly gave place to support for free trade. The unbridling and unprecedented trade growth of the 1950s and 1960s created for Britain a new set of trading circumstances which were prevalent until the oil crises and economic difficulties of the subsequent decade. How did these changes at home and overseas affect the British timber trade? Obviously, the lifting of war-time controls was essential to the operation of a timber trade which could supply all the required species, grades and quantities. Moreover, the extension of free trade agreements between nations lifted artificial barriers like tariffs, although duties on certain manufactured items including plywood remained for a while. Finally, without other countries accepting goods in return for imports to Britain, the drain on the balance of payments and the dollar account – to which timber was a major contributor – would have been impossible to sustain. On the other hand, balance of payments difficulties emerged as endemic to post-war Britain.[3]

The growth in real Gross National Product and consumer spending undoubtedly combined with an easing of trade conditions to stimulate the use of wood. Once more (*see* Chapter III), the construction industry was pivotal. Building investment was depressed between 1948–52 because of the government's determination to stem inflation and a deteriorating balance of payments. In the early 1950s, softwood accounted for three quarters of all timber imports, and some 40 per cent of imported softwood – 30 per cent of all wood arriving at the ports – was destined for the building industry. In response to scarcity, the average amount of timber employed in houses had declined by about a third compared to pre-war usage. Shortages of timber and steel stimulated the construction of pre-fabricated homes and the number of buildings reliant on concrete. As the demand for timber continued to outstrip supply until the mid-1950s, the construction industry did experiment with substitute products, and concrete, used in systemised building techniques, did undermine the timber trade. But the demand for homes adequately compensated for any fall in average usage per building, and the construction companies – like those in the packing case industry, railways, collieries and other substantial users – were soon buying more timber than before the war. In 1951, for example, there were still 750,000 fewer houses than households, and so, by 1956, 2.5m homes were built by the state and private enterprise. During this period, house-building accounted for nearly half of the country's total gross fixed capital investment. Once the government had embarked on a vigorous slum-clearance programme, further developments brought the total to 4.5m by 1963. Within these twelve years, however, the number of households had grown by 2m and many older buildings continued to fall into disrepair. In 1965, some 3m families still lived in slum conditions, to which the state responded by funding local authority construction. Despite improvements in the 1950s and 1960s, homes remained a priority for government social policy and the life ambition of private consumers. Whereas 239,900 houses were built in 1952, 347,800 were finished in 1955. Although the figure declined thereafter, the trend rose from 1958 until it reached 413,700 in 1968. It still stood at 319,300 in 1972.[4]

As controls were lifted in the early to mid-1950s, the packing case industry was – after building – the largest consumer of timber. It was followed by the British Transport Commission's Railway Executive as well as its counterpart at London Transport, and they required sleepers in addition to other construction materials. The National Coal Board maintained a demand for pitwood, and the manufacturers of vehicles, engineering patterns and jigs, furniture, ships, shoe-lathes, coffins, tools, brushes, barrels, and matches all had large raw material needs which had to be met. Although softwood tended to arrive sawn and sometimes planed, the majority of hardwood imports required conversion at sawmills, and most furniture makers – responsible for consuming about one quarter of landed supplies – undertook the task themselves. About one third of all hardwood consumed was home-grown, whereas almost all softwood and plywood was of foreign origin. Moreover, approximately one half of plywood imports went to furniture manufacturers, and a fifth to the building industry.[5]

To meet a rising demand, areas of supply had by the mid-1950s been established or re-established. While imports of softwood from the USSR had declined significantly, Finland and Canada retained their position, and Sweden's role increased. Although hardwoods from Canada and the USA had diminished, tropical countries – notably Ghana and Nigeria – began to exploit their forests and establish indigenous sawmilling industries. Plywood could not be obtained from the Soviet Union in the same quantities as 20 years before, but trade with it, Sweden, and even Germany did slowly revive, and Finland, meanwhile, continued to supply nearly half of Britain's imports. Sawmill operations and throughput gained from dramatic efficiency savings, too. The number of mills in Sweden fell from about 7,000 to 3,600 between 1950 and 1973, while domestic and export output grew from 6.9m to 13.8m cubic metres: in other words, output per unit nearly quadrupled. To cope with the greater throughput there were developments in merchandising. Sawn timber – historically shipped as loose cargo – began to be tied and packaged, and, because ports invested in mechanical lifting-gear, loading and discharging speeds were improved. The leather head and shoulder gear traditionally worn by London dockers to help in the process of manually handling cargoes slowly disappeared. Kiln-drying likewise aided the supply of usable wood to the consumer, as did improvements in inland transport and in shipping links and organisation.

The world output of timber grew from approximately 185m to 310m cubic metres between 1950 and 1973. Canada, which had obtained 26 per cent of the global export market in 1950, retained its primary place with 22 per cent in 1970. Despite fluctuations, Sweden maintained its position with 13 and 12 per cent; Finland

Deal Porter carrying timber at Surrey Commercial Docks, 1949.
Reproduced by permission of the Museum in Docklands, PLA Collection, London.

declined from 12 to 10 per cent; but the Soviet Union expanded its share from 4 to 7 per cent. Austria and the USA were also principal exporters. As for Britain, it could only supply about one twenty-fifth of its needs indigenously. Its imports were subject to frequent fluctuations, but there was a slight rising trend. After the shortages and high inflation rates of the Korean War, importers benefited from a steadily-growing world surplus of timber and falling commodity prices.[6] While Britain landed 9.2m cubic metres in 1953, the total in 1973 reached 15.8. The value of this business still amounted to some 5.2 and 4.1 per cent of all imports, but, in real terms, it hardly altered over two decades.[7] The impact of the diminished use of wood per building and the wider market for man-made substitutes was clearly undermining the trade. The virtual disappearance of the demand for pitwood and wooden barrels also had an impact. During the 1950s, the United States, which, despite its vast forests was not self-sufficient in sawn and planed softwood, emerged as the world's largest importer and Canada's principal market. Japan and the Federal Republic of Germany's inward trade in the commodity overtook that of the United Kingdom (*see* Appendix VII). Finally, in addition to changes in domestic and international demand, the British timber trade underwent other adjustments: although gradually freed in the 1950s from war-time and tariff controls, there was a price to be paid, and that price brought a questioning of the trade's practices and its very structure.

II: RESTRICTIVE PRACTICES, 1952–1960

As we have seen (*see* Chapter III), the restrictive practices which governed the trade in imported timber were formalised in the inter-war period, and were principally designed to protect the role of importers and, to a lesser extent, that of agents. The signing of agreements covering softwood, hardwood and plywood were intended to restrict the number of competitors. Some large users of wood were capable of establishing contacts with producers and shippers, and, in by-passing traditional importers and avoiding their charges, they sought to reduce prices. Moreover, minor buyers could often take advantage of small consignments offered by some shippers at points of landing. During years of over-supply and falling prices, importers were particularly anxious to stabilise trade conditions, and shippers and agents – similarly anxious about potential competitors and the value of their commodity – began to cooperate with the importers. The extension of restrictive practices was, of course, general in British industry and not unusual to the timber trade, and the government took a relaxed, *laissez-faire* attitude to the whole issue. While the United States outlawed combinations and cartels, the British state continued to reject statutory intervention in the economy and generally left the adjudication of trade disputes to common law. During the First World War, the possibility of combinations possibly exploiting shortages and raising prices did raise concern, and the Profiteering Act of 1919 founded a Standing Committee on Trusts to investigate monopolistic activities. The general attitude was, initially, one of genuine enquiry, but, eventually, one of scepticism about the need for state intervention. Indeed, there was open encouragement for the rationalisation of Britain's staple industries and the development of dominant, even oligopolistic corporations which could compete effectively with their American and German counterparts.[8]

The government's general approach to monopolistic practices ensured non-intervention in the 1920s. In any case, fluctuations in the world economy during the inter-war years spurred cut-throat competition and made state interference somewhat superfluous, despite greater trade association activity trying to ameliorate the effect of market difficulties. In the 1930s, the introduction of tariffs and the work of the Import Duties Advisory Committee directly supported monopolistic arrangements. In the timber trade, restrictive arrangements protected by the end of the decade the many small importers and agents against competition from those consumers or shippers interested in becoming importers or wholesale distributors. Changes in public perception and government policy towards restrictive practices occurred during the Second World War, for the economy was controlled to an unprecedented extent and there was an obvious need to plan for decontrol, and to look at issues such as the reintroduction of competition, restrictive practices and collusion. The 1944 White Paper on Employment Policy highlighted the enhanced position of trade associations during the war and hinted that they might be detrimental to economic efficiency, harm long-term employment prospects, and operate against the interests of consumers. War-time controls on timber – particularly as they depended on established firms – and the slowness with which controls were ended after the war strengthened traditional trading links and restrictive practices. Reflecting the government's concern to investigate and improve economic structures, the Industrial Organisation and Development Act was passed in 1947, under which two reports – on the cement and building industries – criticised the influence of restrictive practices. In 1948, the Monopolies and Restrictive Practices (Inquiry and Control) Act reached the statute book: the newly-founded Monopolies and Restrictive Practices Commission could investigate any monopolistic arrangements which affected a third of any industry, and, on its recommendations, the Board of Trade could implement a correcting Order in Council.[9]

The 1948 Monopolies Act was not automatically opposed to restrictive practices, but it did reflect a growing conviction that the public interest was being harmed. It was, nonetheless, hard to be conclusive about the effects of monopolistic practices. The neo-classical theory of the firm favoured freely working markets in which no firm or group of firms was dominant, and it condemned restrictions because they sustained inefficient firms and kept prices artificially high. Another, more recent body of economic literature was equally opposed to any arrangements intended to protect non-viable firms, but it redefined the term efficiency. It argued that oligopolistic units were often needed to reap returns to scale, emphasising how market dominance enabled specialisation and skills in a specific product to be maximised to the benefit of the consumer. While the control of prices and conditions of sale by trade associations could – very obviously – be unfairly used, the unrestricted entry of new, sometimes opportunistic firms and unrestrained price competition might, it was argued, undermine the profitability of firms, weaken the quality of a product or a service, and endanger supplies, particularly of specialist products. The debate often revolved around trade and price instability and their implications for British consumers seeking greater quality and product variety.[10]

During the 1950s, the Monopolies Commission reported on electric lamps, dental goods, cast-iron rainwater products, cables, insulin, copper and copper-based alloys. But it was October 1951 when the Board of Trade referred the Timber Trade Federation and its affiliated associations to the Monopolies Commission. There was, as we have seen, a case to be argued for the retention of restrictive practices – albeit one enjoying falling support – but it was beholden on those being investigated to substantiate their position. The Commission was instructed to report on the key trades in imported softwood, hardwood and plywood, and the Federation formed a special committee to organise a defence.

Although the TTF denied responsibility for the approved lists – they were controlled by its various sections – it was prepared to defend the system, the justification for restrictive practices in all the three cases being the same. The investigators first met the TTF during the following November, and were soon examining its minute books and records. The Commission recognised the Federation to be a loosely-knit organisation, despite having its own secretariat. It represented through its various sections the majority of agents and importers and many non-importing merchants in wholesaling and retailing, and spoke for the whole trade, although no affiliated group was compelled to follow its policies. There was no precise count of firms in the trade as a whole, but there was estimated to be 150 agents, 8–900 importers, and some 1,400 non-importing merchants; 141 agents, about 750 importers, but only some 300 merchants were TTF members. Non-importing merchants were historically not so well represented at the Federation. The affiliated softwood, hardwood and plywood sections were required to fill in three questionnaires about their approved lists during 1952, and the TTF met the Commission in September and once more in 1953 – this time at a public hearing attended by legal counsel – to discuss the Commission's provisional conclusions.

The final *Report on the Supply of Imported Timber* focused upon the three approved lists which governed the relationships between firms in the investigated sections. These lists, as we have seen, contained the names of overseas shippers' agents and United Kingdom importers which agreed to deal only with those placed on the lists. Their control over the timber business was determinant, for 90–5 per cent of all supplies arrived from overseas: the figure for softwood was 95 per cent, that for hardwood 65, and 90 in the case of plywood. Moreover, much of the home-produced plywood was made with imported softwood. Agents, as the representatives of the suppliers and shippers, were undoubtedly crucial to the system of approved lists, and the Swedish Wood Exporters' Association, the Finnish Sawmill Owners' Association, and the Finnish Plywood Manufacturers' Association continued to have a key role in the maintenance of restrictive practices. Many softwood and hardwood agents continued to act as brokers also, and so found customers for unsold landed timber, but the bulk of the business still went through importers and 75–80 per cent of all sales came from their stocks. The importer was expected to purchase a full range of species and sizes, partly to maintain exclusive deals with agents, and partly to be in a position quickly to meet consumer requests. In fact, the role of the importer had increased in recent years, because consumer licensing and import controls had placed complicated procedures in the way of shippers easily supplying an end-user. Many importers did sell directly to consumers, especially in the hardwood trade, as local general merchants might not carry the many specialities required. In all three sections, they might sell to large users or to those close to ports of entry, but most consumer sales were on a small scale and were most easily handled by local wholesalers and retailers. After the war, therefore, the typical timber firm was a small enterprise: there was a plethora of shippers' agents and, by geographical necessity, merchants. Even importers – who could buy and deliver to and from many sources, had to retain stocks, and, in order to meet customer requirements, sometimes engaged in sawmilling operations – had turnovers of less than £100,000 and none controlled more than 10 per cent of either the softwood, hardwood, or plywood trades. Although, incidentally, many importers had interests in timber-using industries, no end-user was an importer, a consequence of the restricted approved list system. Many softwood importers dealt in hardwood also.[11]

The Timber Trade Federation was composed of numerous sections, including representatives of the Timber Development Association, sawmilling, home-grown timber, and local organisations. The Timber Agents' and Brokers' Association and the National Softwood Importers' Section controlled the softwood business; the Hardwood Agents' and Brokers' Association and the Hardwood Importers' Section managed hardwood; and the Plywood Section, with separate sub-sections for agents and importers, oversaw plywood. Almost all agents were members of their respective associations or sub-section, and the rest were in some way connected with the TTF. Importers were less well organised, but, even so, the vast majority were linked to some affiliated association or section.

The TABA and the NSIS continued jointly to elect members of the Softwood Agreement Committee, which controlled entry to the approved list of softwood firms. Admission was granted at the total discretion of the Committee to so-called 'recognised' firms, and all members had to sign a Softwood Sales Agreement, which stipulated that agents and importers should only trade with those on an approved list. The Agreement formally covered only European supplies – a description that omitted the Soviet Union – and it excluded auctions of consignments that were landed unsold.

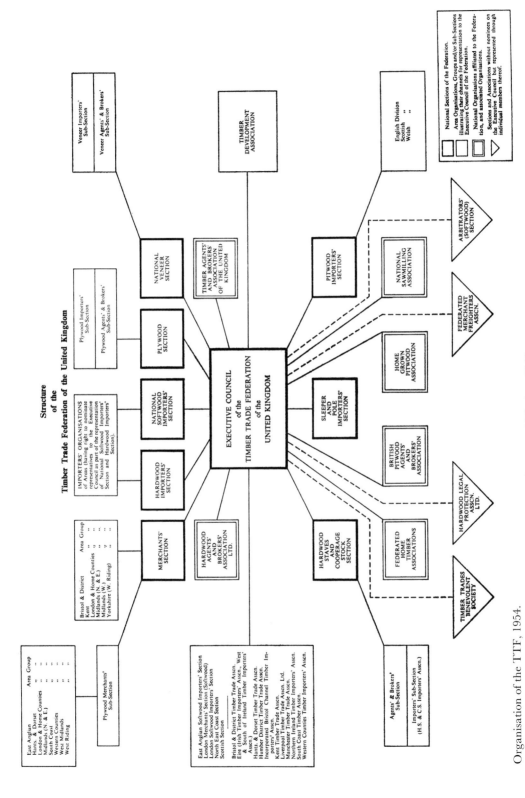

Structure of the Timber Trade Federation of the United Kingdom

Organisation of the TTF, 1954.

Source: Monopolies Commission Report on the Supply of Imported Timber, 1953.

Nonetheless, it did control the bulk of softwood shipments; attempts were being made to extend its terms to North American supplies; and, due to consumer licensing that effectively prohibited unplanned purchases, auctions of unsold stock had effectively ceased.

As in the case of the TABA, all hardwood agents seeking to be members of the HABA had to sign a Hardwood Sales Agreement that set out their obligations under another approved list, then only some three years' old. A Joint Committee, consisting of representatives from the HABA and the Hardwood Importers' Section, managed an approved list whose members had to comply with the Hardwood Agreement. As we have seen, this particular trade had traditionally proved difficult to organise: the influential USA shippers had refused restrictions on their right to sell direct to consumers, and, unlike softwood, there were so many specialities that end-users often preferred to deal with producers themselves. But government restrictions on dollar imports diminished the influence of the USA shippers in the British hardwood trade, and enabled the approved list drawn up before the war finally to become operative in 1950. The main purpose of the Hardwood Agreement was to halt direct selling by shippers. But the Agreement accepted the complexities of its trade, and allowed signatories to deal outside the approved list so long as terms and final prices were compatible. Certain goods such as shuttle blocks, birch and maple squares for textile bobbins, and pieces for the internal workings of pianos had historically depended on direct contracts with shippers' agents, and in effect were untouched by the Hardwood Agreement. Moreover, unlike the Softwood Agreement, hardwood importers could sell direct to consumers, since non-importing merchants would not necessarily stock all the different specialities.

The Joint Committee of the Plywood Section retained oversight of its Agents' and Importers' Sub-Sections, and had sole authority over membership of an approved list. Some types of timber imports, of course, were not controlled in any way by approved lists. Sleepers were handled by 14 importers which bought direct from the shippers and sold to the Railway and London Transport Executives. Boxboards, made of softwood and cut to size, and coopers' staves were imported by the end-users which dealt with shippers' agents. Finally, the National Coal Board continued to organise its own supply of pitwood.[12]

The 1953 *Report* stressed that the approved lists were not formally used to fix commission charges and prices. Although the standard contracts urged upon favoured firms tended to set price boundaries, they were not generally regarded as obligatory. One exception was the plywood trade, where standard contracts restricted commissions to the 5 per cent set by the war-time Timber Control. Furthermore, a handful of local associations representing non-importing merchants organised price-fixing, although the practice, limited to a few rural areas, was in decline. There were no known instances of firms fixing quotas between themselves. In brief, the development of competition from firms outside the approved lists was restrained, but competition did occur between those named on the lists. The approved lists ensured that timber transactions passed through both an agent and an importer, and recognition as an agent or importer was consequently restricted. Conditions of entry to either trade remained substantially the same as those agreed in pre-war years. Undoubtedly, most end-users believed that prices were competitive, and supported the role of the importer. By the nature of their trade, builders moved from site to site and could not hold large stocks of wood. Competition and fluctuations in demand prevented them tying up large levels of capital. Builders – who bought the largest proportion of softwood – sought to buy their specific requirements whenever needed, and preferred it to arrive made ready for use by the importer or merchant. They had neither the resources nor the inclination to deal directly with shippers.

Other consumers, however, wanted the use of importers whenever necessary but freedom to import whenever it was more convenient, and furniture and box-making firms were particularly vociferous in their condemnation of restricted practices. The biggest makers of furniture – large users of hardwood and plywood – had often dealt with shippers before the war, but could no longer do so. They still had to explain their requirements to suppliers, visited them regularly, and believed that their buyers were as expert as any importer. Some packing-case firms had before the war purchased nearly all their wood direct, and the Timber Trade Federation had refused them entry on to the approved list of plywood importers. They were additionally aggrieved that some established importers had manufacturing plywood operations and that they could, as a consequence of restrictive practices, produce their boxes more cheaply. Both the furniture and box industries believed that their costs had increased with the increasing scope of restrictive practices during the war and the period of control. Non-importing merchants barred from the approved lists not surprisingly had reasons for resentment, especially when they held Board of Trade import licences and were then refused supplies by agents. There was a question also of natural justice: the reasons for refusal were not clear nor subject to public scrutiny.

Although competition did occur amongst favoured firms, it was clear to the Monopolies Commission that the levels of competition were delineated to some extent by the restrictions placed upon the numbers of agents and importers. After all, the system was intended to stabilise trading conditions, and the tie of mutual interests amongst members of the approved list did exist. By restricting the right of merchants and others to become importers, the trade was preventing investment and the development of more economical channels of trade. The 1953 *Report* concluded that, if the approved list system were removed, the importers would only lose a small proportion of their trade, and that the nature of their business was already diverse and required flexibility. The Commission asserted that competition from new firms would provide a healthy stimulus and that, therefore, the approved lists were contrary to the public interest.[13]

As a consequence of the *Report*, the Minister of Materials, Lord Woolton, met representatives of the Timber Trade Federation in November 1953. The TTF attacked the *Report* for its ideological objection to restrictive practices, but the government's position was non-negotiable: Woolton insisted on talking about how the trade would end the approved list system, and would not debate the Commission's conclusion. Faced with the choice of voluntary compliance or the force of a government Order, the President of the TTF, Frank Urmston, in January 1954 announced that all the Sections would comply rather than have an Order imposed, although they continued to dispute the *Report*. By the following month, the National Softwood Importers' Section and the Hardwood Importers' Section had abrogated their approved list agreements. The Plywood Section complied in March, yet, with the plywood trade under the control of the 'big six' importers, little change was expected. Although the Hardwood Agents' and Brokers' Association and the Hardwood Importers' Section dissolved the joint committee responsible for their approved list in May 1954, they retained a liaison committee which at its first meeting urged that the structure of the trade be preserved. In September, the Timber Agents' and Brokers' Association and the National Softwood Importers' Association reminded its members that all restrictive agreements had been withdrawn, but similarly urged that normal channels be retained. More to the point, all three parts of the timber trade had replaced the approved lists with lists of recommended names. To comply with the Commission's terms, the various associations and sections of the TTF could no longer bind its members to do business only with favoured firms, but they could circulate the names of those which were preferred or 'reputable'. In October, the Board of Trade – which had assumed the Ministry of Material's supervision of the timber trade – wrote to the TTF's President, Frank Uranston, about the new lists and statements of policy, and asked for assurances that restricted practices were not being resurrected in a different form. But, at a succession of meetings and private dinners, the softwood and hardwood trade was urged to retain traditional trading practices, the Federation taking the view that by merely withdrawing the approved lists it was complying with the 1953 *Report*. The plywood business, more closely-knit, did not even require recommended lists.[14]

Despite forthcoming assurances, the government remained suspicious of trade practices amongst timber firms, and policy on the whole issue, indeed, hardened throughout the 1950s. Following a report demonstrating the prevalence of trade agreements, the government passed the Restrictive Trade Practices Act in 1956. Investigations carried out by the Monopolies Commission since its founding had concluded that restrictive practices were contrary to the public interest, and so sought through their registration the legal testing of their validity. The Act concerned all agreements between two or more firms on prices, quotas, conditions of sale, approved lists, and monopolistic arrangements. Administrative control through the Monopolies Commission was replaced by a process of judicial review before the Restrictive Trade Practices Court, whose remit was more sceptical about many established arrangements and required their participants to prove their value. The Act, therefore, was intended to be a general attack on restrictive practices.[15]

The TTF had to decide on its strategy towards the new legislation. It was possible to reintroduce all the abrogated agreements and register them with the Court prior to formal judgment. Unfortunately for the TTF, such a course of action was not open to any trade that had already been investigated within the last three years, and, in any case, success was far from certain. The Federation faced the inevitable in February 1957: on the advice of lawyers, the softwood and hardwood sections withdrew the lists of recommended firms that had replaced the previous approved system. When, in February 1958, the Monopolies and Restrictive Practices Court announced another investigation into the timber business, it was particularly interested in possible breaches of assurances following the withdrawal of approved lists. After an initial hearing in March, a TTF delegation and counsel met the Board of Trade in May to defend themselves. The subsequent *Report*, published in 1958, did not dispute that the approved lists had been abrogated some four years but concluded that the recommendations subsequently sent to firms, meetings, and trade dinners had created mutual obligations for nearly four years thereafter. The recommendations sent out must have been agreed, it was concluded, and, particularly in the hardwood trade, meetings and dinners had been used to persuade firms to hold the line. The TTF replied that all decisions were reached voluntarily, but the Commission argued that the 'real sanction for any arrangement of this kind, whether formally provided for or not, is in the known existence of a substantial body of common opinion in the trade', and that many in the trade felt the force of that sanction. The 1958 *Report* continued: 'it remains true that certain persons are prevented from doing business in the way they would wish principally because their names, or their customers' names, are not included in the lists recognised by the main bodies of importers or agents, and we think the effects of the arrangements which we find to have existed as regards hardwood and softwood have been and are similar to those of former agreements'. It was the hardwood trade – because it experienced historically the greatest instance of direct dealing between consumer and shipper – which had striven most to retain some system of 'recommended' firms.[16] Following discussions in 1959 between the Board of Trade, the Registrar of Restrictive Trades Agreements, and the TTF, it was ordered that the rules and regulations of the Federation be registered. As a result, the Court reviewed the recommended list systems in the softwood and hardwood businesses, and, in August 1960, both were declared illegal. The Registrar also became interested in the activities of the Plywood Section, but enquiries were complicated by the absence of any formal arrangements amongst the small number of well connected firms.[17]

What impact did the Monopolies Commission *Report* in 1953 and the 1956 Act have upon the organisation of the timber trade? There was little criticism about price collusion: although established practice often guided commission rates, the industry's many small-scale firms were allowed to compete within the approved lists system. In any case, they all dealt in an internationally-traded commodity, and, in general, prices were not within their control. The restrictive practices – designed, depending on one's view, to stabilise or protect the timber trade – were a separate matter. The earlier investigation, conducted by the Monopolies Commission, wanted an end to approved lists, yet recognised that most importers would only be marginally affected by any change, simply because the number of consumers which could deal directly with shippers was limited. The second enquiry was eventually certain, nonetheless, that the replacement of 'approved' by 'recommended' lists and the existence of unwritten agreements maintained restrictive practices. It is more difficult to judge whether the ending of agreements in all forms had a significant impact on the structure and the nature of the timber business after 1960. Undoubtedly, opinion within the trade saw the Commission's decision as unnecessary and most firms, therefore, remained sceptical about its impact. A minority, on the other hand, viewed it as a watershed in industrial organisation.[18] It is true that subsequent restructuring in the following decade did undermine divisions along functional lines, but there were organisational and commercial reasons which helped create this impetus. Nevertheless, the work of the Monopolies Commission both removed any artificial barriers to these developments, and established a climate of opinion against restrictive practices.

III: RESTRUCTURING, 1960–1973

The Commission, in other words, forced the timber trade to confront the inevitable, perhaps at an earlier date than it would have achieved if free of legislative interference. The TTF in 1959 began to discuss its own internal organisation and the very structure of the trade itself. The Federation, after all, had acted as an umbrella organisation for the various sections that had administered the approved lists. The maintenance of restrictive practices had emerged in the 1950s as the TTF's principal task, and, in the absence of a list system, the Federation had to answer questions about its purpose. But, of course, any new organisation had to suit the emerging trade structure and conditions. In October 1959, Sir Harold Emmerson, formerly Permanent Secretary at the Ministry of Labour, was appointed to lead an investigation into the TTF and the Timber Development Association's constitutions. He was asked, in addition, to advise on future finances, research, publicity, membership, and relations with the timber-consumer industries. Only 10 per cent of firms responded to forwarded questionnaires, but Emmerson reported in 1960, highlighting a general presumption that there were too many firms engaged in import and distribution. The development of new materials had undermined the timber trade, and softwood consumption stood at about 70 per cent of pre-war quantities. As the number of firms had not fallen, returns were considered poor, and low profitability and the small-scale nature of operations had left companies undercapitalised and unable to compete adequately against the new materials. The Emmerson Report urged the TTF to guide the necessary process of rationalisation. He pointed out an initial movement towards bigger units: the development of the general builder's merchant was already affecting the distribution of timber. The TTF – which for so long had concentrated on the interests of agents and importers – could no longer overlook the indigenous industry. The Forestry

Commission was emerging as a major force, and the Federated Home Timber Associations already had 549 members, 100 of whom were linked to the TTF. The report also considered the role of non-importing merchants, and wanted the involvement of timber consumers too. In other words, the Federation had in future to be more than an organisation which maintained restrictive practices for the benefit of agents and importers. Emmerson argued for a reduction in the number of member associations, and replacement of the cumbersome Executive Council by a representative Council and a more effective Executive Committee. A new Director General was envisaged as head of a more streamlined organisation, and the TTF was asked to take on the tasks of information, publicity and trade advertising. The financing of the Trade Development Association remained problematic, however; members were uncertain of the benefits and relations with the Department of Scientific and Industrial Research were difficult. During the previous decade, the government had funded timber research and divided work between the TDA and the DSIR. When the Department sought to concentrate all activity at Princes Risborough, it wanted the Forestry Commission's Forest Products Research Laboratory to deal with the areas previously handled by the TDA.[19]

In the event, the TTF decided against creating a post of Director General, but it did in October 1961 appoint Sir John Simpson as its salaried chairman, who remained in his post for over four years. At an Extraordinary General Meeting held in December, however, the TTF did follow Emmerson's recommendation and formed a separate Executive Committee and Council. By 1963, the Trade Development Association had reached an agreement with the DSIR, and, granted affiliated status, was renamed the Timber Research and Development Association.[20]

These changes in the TTF organisation and objectives did not adequately tackle some of the important issues raised by Emmerson about the future of the timber trade, particularly changes in market structure and the need for larger firms. The traditional agents and importers once dominant in the British trade were by the early 1960s beginning to be displaced by sales subsidiaries founded by the bigger Swedish exporters. The Swedes were soon being imitated by the Finnish, Canadians and Americans. It was a trend which in the main, undermined the role of agents, but, with sales increasingly being made direct to consumers, importers also. As shippers sought to entrench their sales and marketing operations, they bought British timber firms in the furtherance of horizontal integration. Developments in merchanting – the packaging of exported timber – and the greater use of mechanical lifting at ports both encouraged shippers to organise the delivery of timber from source to end-use. Exporters began to open their own terminals and carry timber in bulk carriers. They sought to exploit new returns to scale and saw marketing advantages in dealing directly with consumers. As a result, activities once left to importers such as stress grading and kiln drying were to an increasing extent carried out overseas. Some importers and merchants sought to gain the advantages of greater throughput and centrally-coordinated distribution planning, but in general the response of the British

James Latham timber yard, 1966.
Courtesy of James Latham Plc, Clapton, London.

trade in the 1960s was seen as slow. But new groups which operated throughout the whole country did emerge, and many firms moved into the expanding plywood trade. Horizontal extensions of business, moreover, were accompanied by vertical extensions of function, although to a more limited extent. While the agent and importer were being challenged and undoubtedly changing their functional roles, the non-importing merchant, sawmilling and processing operations, and building firms often retained their specific occupations. The TTF Council in 1966 acknowledged general developments in the pattern and organisation of UK trade. The Board of Trade was at the time looking into import restrictions, and the Labour Government's National Plan was critical of the small size of many British companies. Given the country's balance of payments difficulties and the high levels of currency expended upon timber, the trade was soon subjected to renewed investigation. The lack of scale economies was easy to illustrate: of the 6–700 timber importers, some 27 accounted for 50 per cent of all imports; and numbers of softwood importers had hardly changed – at around 400 – for 30 years.[21]

By the early 1970s, the trade was more willing to accept the implications of these structural changes. It was accepted that British firms needed to merge and consolidate, and that the industry had to counter the increasing use of ferrous-concrete. But the trade remained highly fragmented and the Timber Trade Federation's constitution and the continuing role of its sections reflected this reality.[22] The rationalisation of so many firms with varied competitive and trading interests was, to no surprise, difficult to achieve. Coordinated action involving the British trade against overseas companies and the manufacturers of substitute materials seemed even more unrealistic. In 1972, the TTF decided to commission another report, which would – like its predecessor ten or so years before – investigate the constitution of the Federation, trade structure, rationalisation, and the future of timber as a raw material. Having ceased to be an organisation concentrating upon restrictive practices and the sectoral interests of agents and importers, the TTF had failed to gain a new role. Whether the Federation and the trade would be able to respond to changing circumstances was an open question, and the more difficult condition of world trade in the 1970s soon made the problem an acute one.

REFERENCES

1 W. Ashworth, *A Short History of the World Economy since 1850*, 1964, pp.266–8, 270–1, 275; J. Foremen-Peck, *A History of the World Economy: International Economic Relations since 1850*, 1983, pp.262–3, 267–9, 273–5, 298–9, 331–45; H. van der Wee, *Prosperity and Upheaval: the World Economy, 1945–1980*, 1991, pp.258–80, 345–89.

2. Ibid., TTF, Council Minutes, 17 June 1959.

3. Cf. Mitchell, 1990.

4. G.O. Allen, 'The Building Industry' in *British Industries and their Organisation*, 1959, pp.295, 311; P. Gregg, *The Welfare State*, 1967, pp.231–33; Mitchell, 1990, p.390; M. Bowley, 1966, pp.104–86, 199–290, 396–464.

5. *Report . . .*, 1953, pp.5–9; M. Bowley, *Innovations in Building Materials*, 1960, pp.134–143.

6. Latham, 1957, pp.71–75; Interviews with L.C.L. Groth, 1 Nov 1991; and L.A. Woodburn-Bamberger, 3 Oct 1991. Imports by country of consignment before and after the war and controls were:

Softwood %	1938	1955
Finland	27.7	25.6
Canada	22.5	19.0
Poland	6.6	3.1
Sweden	18.9	27.0
USA	2.0	0.8
USSR	25.2	14.3
Hardwood %		
Canada	18.0	4.9
USA	34.0	3.0
Ghana	1.3	14.8
Nigeria	3.1	21.0
Plywood %		
Finland	44.4	46.8
USSR	32.7	17.0

7. TTF, *U.K. Year Book of Timber Statistics, 1983–85*, p.4.

8. Hannah, 1983, pp.43–5.

9. C. Brock, *The Control of Restrictive Practices from 1956*, 1966, pp.20–38; *Report*, 1953, pp.72–9.

10. Brock, 1966, pp.1–19.

11. *Report . . .*, 1953, pp.1–3, 10–15, 19–24, 64; *Report*, 1958, p.8; Latham, 1965, p.143; TTF, Executive Council, 20 May 1953.

12. *Report . . .*, 1953, pp.19–39, 46–8, 51–4, 72–9. The number of affiliated firms were: NSIS, 500 members (there were in addition 50–60 not in NSIS but in the TTF, and about 60 in neither); 110 in TABA; the Plywood Agents' Sub-Section, 67 (only one agent was not a member); Plywood Importers' Sub-Section, 97; HABA, 82 (including 67 that also imported softwood); the Hardwood Importers' Section, 251.

13. *Report . . .*, 1953, pp.15–6, 55–7, 60–3, 67, 72–9; Latham, 1957, pp.143–6.

14. *Report . . .*, 1958, pp.5–23; Latham, 1953, p.146; TTF Council, 2, 17 Dec 1953; 6 June 1954.

15. Brock, 1965, pp.38–62; K.D. George, *Industrial Organisation: Competition, Growth, and Structural Changes in Britain, 1975*, pp.146–192.

16. *Report . . .*, 1958, pp.1–4, 8, 24–8, 40–57; TTF Council, 21 Sept 1955, 30 May 1956, 20 Feb 1957, 19 Feb 1958, 17 June 1958.

17. Latham, 1957, pp.154, 156; TTF, Council, 8 June 1960, 14 Feb 1961, 8 Dec 1965, 16 Feb 1966.

18. Interviews with G.N. Donaldson, 3 Oct 1991; T.S. Mallinson, 3 Oct 1991; R.E. Groves, C.B.E., 3 Oct 1991; E.M.L. Latham, 30 Oct 1991; L.A. Woodburn-Bamberger, 3 Oct 1991; J.G. Wright, 10 Oct 1991.

19. H. Emmerson, *Report on the Organisation of the TTF of the UK and the TDA*, 1960, pp.2–4, 11, 13–14, 19–25, 155, 157–9; Latham, 1965, pp.152–6; TTF, Council, 18 Feb 1959, 17 June 1959, 21 Oct 1959.

20. Emmerson Report, pp.152, 159–62; TTF, Council, 18 Oct 1961, 13 Dec 1961, 27 June 1962; TTF, Council, 8 Dec 1965; B. Fraser, *Report on the T.T.F.*, 1973, pp.1–4.

21. TTF, Council, 12 Oct 1966, 7 Dec 1966; Swedish Wood Exporters' Association, *The Centenary of the Swedish Wood Exporters, 1875–1975: Developments from 1950 to 1975*, 1975, pp.8–9, 20–1, 24–5, 38–9, 72–3; Interviews with T.S. Mallinson, 3 Oct 1991; R.E. Groves, C.B.E., 3 Oct 1991; E.M.L. Latham, 30 Oct 1991; L.A. Woodburn-Bamberger, 3 Oct 1991; J.G. Wright, 10 Oct 1991; L.C.L. Groth, 1 Nov 1991.

22. Fraser Report, pp.1–4.

— V —
CRISES OF
COMMODITIES,
1973–1992

I: ECONOMIC CONDITIONS AND TRADE STRUCTURE, 1973–1979

I n the two decades after 1973, the timber trade had to face a succession of crises. Although many of its ensuing problems were experienced by various sectors of the economy, they had a particular impact on an imported commodity like timber. In the 1970s, the trade encountered the common problems of slowed growth and rapid inflation. But it remained, in addition, vulnerable to cheaper substitutes, and, during the following decade, the trade was hurt by a sharp fall in house building. Later, timber became the object of ecological concern, and ethical and environmental questions about logging operations and levels of timber consumption – about the very position of timber as a viable and sustainable commodity – began to be publicly debated. In dealing with and answering all these threats to the business, the TTF had an obvious role. In order to suppress inflation, the government in the 1970s assumed control of prices and incomes, and, as a consequence, it encouraged relations between itself and trade associations. The practice and results of these contacts, however, were eventually disappointing. The Federation, together with TRADA, spearheaded the industry's defence against man-made timber substitutes. Finally, the Federation sought to persuade public opinion that timber was imported and sold by ecologically responsible traders. Whether, however, the TTF on its own was powerful or influential enough to counter the environmentalist campaign continued to be an unresolved question.

Changes in economic conditions and government policies after 1973 directly affected the timber trade. Alterations to the world trading patterns that had emerged after the Second World War had to be accommodated. The less developed countries of the southern hemisphere – including the tropical hardwood exporters – began to challenge the existing system of international trade institutions. Arguing that they had had no part in the shaping of post-war commercial relations, these nations asserted that the expansion of free trade had disproportionately benefited the more economically powerful West. In a world divided between the exporters and importers of primary products, a system of free trade had seemingly enabled industrialised countries to determine commodity prices and output levels. As a result, many primary product exporters began to press for increased development funds and the relocation of industrial production within their own borders. In the hope of controlling price and output levels, they also formed international cartels. The Organisation of Petroleum Exporting Countries – since it controlled the most strategic of resources – was the most notable example, and the rise of oil prices in October 1973 had a direct impact on global economic activity. The effect on Britain's balance of payments was patent. But, on the whole, most cartel arrangements ultimately failed.

Governments, too, became more willing to intervene and determine the terms of international trade. The 1975 Lome Convention between the European Community and associated African, Caribbean, and Pacific states, for example, sought to guarantee earnings from 12 major commodities. As a result of these many developments, the 1970s was marked by a change in the conditions of international trade, largely due to a steep rise in commodity prices. Unfortunately for the less developed countries concerned, the benefits they gained from price increases, cartels and trade agreements were all too often of a partial or temporary nature. Inflationary pressures damaged the very demand for commodities. Moreover, many industrialised countries attempted – as in the Multi-Fibre Arrangement – to protect their indigenous industries from cheaper overseas products and rising raw material costs, and adopted import quotas and subsidies. The European Community's Generalised Scheme of Preferences was established to allow an annual quota of duty-free plywood, ostensibly to assist developing nations. In fact, the German and French industries were best placed to gain advantage. Furthermore, the UK received most of its plywood imports from the Commonwealth, and these had in the past been accepted free of duty. Under the GSP, they become subject to tariffs once the agreed quota had been filled. Such an arrangement also aggravated price instability in an already volatile market, but, notwithstanding these particular difficulties, the trade in sheet materials – namely, plywood, chipboard, and fibre building board – became a business with major growth potential.[1]

Challenges to the liberal world trade order, falling output, and rising commodity prices naturally affected Britain and its timber business. As a trading nation, the country was dependent upon exports which paid for imports of food and raw materials. Although the advantages in economic growth and specialisation seemed apparent, the expansion of world trade after the Second World War had accentuated this dependence, and balance of payments crises were, as a consequence, a recurring feature of British economic life. The country was especially vulnerable to any lack of demand for its manufactured exports, and it was dogged by an external constraint that induced governments to resort on a regular basis to deflationary measures. Often using the crude instrument of higher interest rates, governments suppressed domestic demand in the hope of reducing the import bill. As export growth continued to slow, it became clear that some bolder initiative was needed and that sterling's exchange rate was fixed at too high a level. In a move expected to boost exports and correct a negative balance of payments, the pound was devalued from a level of $2.80 to $2.40 in 1967. If the decision gained the support of major exporters, it hurt the fortunes of importers such as the timber trade, whose commodities became more expensive by nearly 17 per cent overnight. In 1972, Britain followed the United States, ended fixed exchange rates and established a floating currency. Whatever the long-standing problems of the British economy, it is arguable that the balance of payments gap did not emerge as a major difficulty until the 1970s. Britain faced the problems of worldwide recession at the beginning of the decade, but budgetary policies introduced when world circumstances were changing helped produce an inflationary boom in 1972 and 1973. As a consequence, the Conservative government reintroduced the prices and incomes policies it had abolished on taking office from the previous Labour administration. It sought to control inflation and raise productivity, but certain 'push' factors – namely a continuous rise in commodity prices after 1973 – defeated its attempts. The sense of crisis, nonetheless, led the Labour governments after 1974 to retain income and price restraints. While inflation in Britain had once been only slightly above that of major competitors, it became explosive, and, furthermore, linked at times to falling output and a deteriorating balance of payments. Although there was some easing of the position in the mid-1970s and an improvement in economic growth, commodity and oil prices began to rise again in 1979.[2]

The inflationary budget of 1971 and the subsequent property boom proved an undoubted boon to the timber trade. Indeed, throughout the 1970s, housing and the market for building materials were affected by inflationary pressures of demand as well as supply, the need for homes and the wish for home-ownership greatly exceeding supply. Government grants also stimulated a trend in home improvements. This growth in domestic demand coincided with rising worldwide needs, and British importers, hampered by the recent consequences of devaluation, had to trade in a competitive market. At the zenith of the economic boom in 1973, 'gazumping' in some areas of supply – in most cases the hardwood trade – became common practice. Foreign shippers fell behind in supplying their importer customers, and, as prices rose, some were unable to complete contracts at the agreed price; alternatively, as they sought higher payments from their original or another importer, they were tempted to ignore existing contracts. It was true that Far Eastern traders and state marketing organisations in Eastern Europe – but not the USSR – had historically engaged in the practice, but the problem worsened during these years of rapid price inflation. Contract difficulties and supply problems were compounded by bad weather and labour troubles in Canada. During 1973, the wholesale price of wood imported into Britain rose by nearly 57 per cent.[3]

The President of the TTF, L.A. Woodburn-Bamberger, in 1974, denied any imminent worldwide shortage.[4] There was a plentiful supply of trees in areas of logging operations as well as untapped forests, but processing and transport resources

105

had become overstretched. The TTF declined to make public pronouncements on timber prices or supplies. The Executive Committee did not feel it had the authority to take collective action, even over a serious matter such as 'gazumping'. Firms were left to act on their own. In any case, by 1974, the situation had been completely reversed: the Government credit squeeze had left many UK companies in financial distress, and importers tried to delay or make changes in contracts. The experience was a graphic reminder of the timber trade's cyclical nature. Boom periods, with too much timber arriving at the ports were followed by high stock holdings; high prices and falling demand required adjustment from both shippers and importers. The oil and commodity crisis, the three day week and sterling problems added to the difficulties of importers. The construction industry, which still accounted for 70 per cent of timber consumption, was badly affected by the country's economic difficulties: by 1974, the quantity of timber imported was some 20 per cent down over the previous year, and softwood stocks had grown by 57 per cent.[5] Prices, consequently, fell in 1975. Amongst these difficulties, there were some redeeming features. As long as there was an oil crisis, timber would benefit from being one of the lowest consumers of energy, while manufactured and processed substitutes were fuel-hungry. Production was growing in traditional areas such as Africa, Canada and Russia, and Latin America also showed promise as a major supplier.[6] But in 1976, a fall in the value of the pound – from just over $2 to just over $1.70 – forced up timber prices in sterling terms. Following criticism of the trade's structure and practices, *The Times* reported a rumour that the Monopolies Commission was to investigate timber prices, but it proved ill-founded. This seemed ironic to the timber trade, which already felt burdened by the Price Code. Some relief was afforded by official revision in 1976, when the TTF pointed out the cyclical nature of the trade and emphasised the need for retained profits if forward commitments and stocks were to be financed.

The economic vicissitudes of the 1970s put pressures on costs, strained the timber industry's structure and led to further mergers, take-overs and combinations. But greater efficiency also resulted from improvements in transportation, packaging and handling, while port facilities continued to be extended. Agents no longer necessarily specialised in a particular kind of timber, but had to deal with all types, and work for shippers throughout the world. Importing firms or groups became larger too, greater turnover per unit emerging as an important contributor to competitive advantage and survival. The blurring of traditional lines of demarcation between importers, merchants, and wholesale and retail outlets was hastened by the general economic difficulties. Importers became importer-merchants and took over retail businesses, while some of the larger groups bought agent firms. Overseas shippers set up operations to import and sell their products in the UK. Customers became more demanding, and merchants had to provide more choice and stock new products such as chipboard and fibreboard. The re-formed larger groups, for example, Meyer-Southern-Evans and William Mallinson-Denny Mott, obtained advantages in buying, distribution and manufacturing. Dominant groups such as Meyer International, Hunter, Harcross and Travis Perkins emerged in the following decade. In other cases, small family firms like George Donaldson and Sons of Scotland diversified into manufacturing or fabrication, and formed subsidiary companies. On the retailing side, firms set up their own self-service outlets, stocking, together with timber, other materials for building and home improvement. Some built their own wharves and sawmills and began dealing in all types of wood, both imported and home grown.

While the trade emerged as more 'commodity' than 'sectionally-oriented', the TTF's organisation did not reflect this change, and, as the industry rationalised, the Area Associations became less relevant. As we have seen, there appeared to be a growing role for trade associations, first with the foundation of the National Economic Development Council in 1962 with its talk of industrial strategy, and latterly as a result of the Labour Government's National Plan and price and income controls. In 1970, 70 companies – largely within the Confederation of British Industry – had formed a Commission of Inquiry into Industrial Representation, headed by Lord Devlin. It reported within two years, arguing that the UK's 2,000 or so trade associations were poorly funded and generally too small to have any impact upon government policy. The Commission noted that following the ending of restrictive practices in 1956 and 1964, several associations had failed to find a new role. It stressed that organisations such as the TTF should, in future, seek to provide essential services for its members. These included the monitoring of government policy and legislation, the provision of legal and economic advice, technical publications, trade missions, exhibitions, and cooperation with the British Standards Institute, which was promoting more economical use of imported materials such as timber. The Timber Trade Federation represented some three-quarters of all firms dealing in imported woods, and these in turn were responsible for distributing 85 per cent of all timber volumes consumed. There were 64 trade associations or employers' organisations within the timber and furniture industries, and the Devlin Report urged the trade to establish a more unitary body with a structure better suited for providing advice, information, and joint action. The Report, moreover, wanted trade associations to be more effective in their lobbying of government.[7]

The Timber Trade Federation responded by asking Sir Bruce Fraser, KCB, formerly Comptroller and Auditor General (1966–71) in the Exchequer and Audit Department, to investigate its structure in 1972. In addition, government proposals to phase out, over the next ten years, general research grants to organisations such as TRADA and replace them with selective support for specific projects had direct implications for the Federation, its organisation and financing. As previously noted, TTF members automatically became members of TRADA, which absorbed most of the Federation's membership fees, and there was growing concern over what many in the Federation saw as the Association's lack of accountability. Fraser reported in 1973, recommending that individual firms should apply directly to the TTF for membership and not by way of its various sections. Members would then be put on one or more of three Registers covering agents, importers or merchants. The Federation

Headquarters of TRADA, Stocking Lane, Hughenden Valley, High Wycombe.
Courtesy of TRADA.

had to face the challenges of the future, namely product standardisation, more processing and the manufacture of pre-fabricated joinery, and competition from substitute materials. There was, in addition, an international role for the Federation in encouraging overseas supplying countries to demonstrate good management of timber resources.

In contrast to the outcome of the Emmerson Report a decade earlier, Fraser's recommendation for a full-time Director General was accepted, Sydney Redman, C.B., former Under-Secretary of State at the Ministry of Defence, becoming the first incumbent in 1973. The Report advocated the streamlining of the TTF Council and strongly supported TRADA's role within the industry, since the battle against substitutes rested on its success. Finance and subscriptions proved thorny issues, but direct membership, new rules and revised contributions all came into force in January 1974. Although member firms joined the TTF itself, five divisions dealing with importers, agents, merchants, international members, and sawmillers were formed. Area Associations continued and had representation on the Council and appropriate committees. Company subscriptions were replaced by levies based on the previous year's sales and were used to fund TRADA as well as the TTF.[8]

The changing trading conditions and the expansion of government into the business community appeared to herald an enhanced role for trade associations in government business negotiations. But, like the plans which in 1962 had underpinned the formation of the National Economic Development Council, and discussion of a National Plan and economic strategy between 1964–6, any need for tripartite cooperation in economic planning eventually disappeared. On the issue of incomes policy and price controls between 1966 and 1974, the Confederation of British Industry consistently opposed statutory measures, but was reluctantly forced to follow government initiatives, the CBI only affecting the details of policy and not its broad direction. Business' experience of the Labour Government's voluntary pay restraint and prices policies after 1974 was similar and representations from trade associations had little impact. On the return of the Conservatives to power in 1979, the emphasis on minimal state intervention and trust in market-oriented solutions augured, not a break with the past, but the homecoming of a traditional viewpoint. Although incomes and pay policies had been an ever-present reality for nearly 15 years, economic and industrial planning was never materially pursued. On questions of interest rates, exchange policy, and taxation, political imperatives were, as always, decisive.[9]

Following consideration of the Fraser Report, the Timber Trade Federation was reorganised at the beginning of 1974 to accommodate presumptions about the enhanced political role of trade associations, yet this potential new role did not – as we have seen – actually replace its lost involvement in restrictive practices. The TTF, therefore, would have to prove effective at delivering services that its member companies found useful or essential and which they could not supply themselves. The Federation, in other words, would have to be effective in providing advice and information, co-ordinating research and development, and promoting timber.

Balance of payments difficulties during the 1970s influenced the nature of the timber trade in one marginal way: it re-awakened interest in home-grown supplies, and a White Paper on Forestry Policy was published in 1972. The government wanted to reduce the import bill by 10 per cent. High prices and rising unemployment strengthened the case for indigenous forests, and, as substitutes like concrete and plastics were high energy consumers, the fuel and oil crisis was also influential in policy initiatives. 55 acres per annum would be allocated for planting and replanting, making the previous target of 5m acres of productive woodlands by the year 2000 unrealistic (*see* Chapter 3). Despite the government's continuing interest in home-grown supplies, timber production remained at modest levels, although technical developments, especially the introduction of chippers and the modernisation of sawmilling, facilitated the greater utilisation of trees and their residues. By 1985, only 12 per cent of the UK's timber needs were met through indigenous supplies.[10] The failure to achieve the new planting and replanting targets in both Forestry Commission and privately owned woodlands was a disappointment but, by the end of the 1980s, reform of the European Community's Common Agricultural Policy did release funds for afforestation. Funding, originally at £46m in 1989, was set to rise to £131m by 1992.[11]

Although the energy crisis of the early 1970s had briefly reawakened interest in timber over substitutes, the long-term trend continued to undermine wood usage (*see* Appendix III). However, the timber trade was still a large-scale importer of an, albeit essential, commodity that contributed extensively to Britain's balance of payments problems. It had to tackle the problems of economic cycles, exchange fluctuations and inflation, and profitability had suffered as a result. But substitutes probably constituted the greater danger to the future of the business. The Timber Trade Federation and the Timber Research and Development Association held responsibility for coordinating a response. TRADA's role, however, was the subject of debate within the Federation: should an organisation, traditionally a technical research establishment, take on advertising and public relations?

II: RESEARCH AND MARKET DEVELOPMENT IN THE 1970S AND 1980S

When TRADA published its pamphlet *Objectives for Timber Development in the 1970s*, it set out an ambitious programme of research and education, yet lack of finance from government and industry sources remained a major constraint on its objectives. Many members of the TTF criticised TRADA's emphasis on pure research and, instead, wanted an increase in promotion and advice to timber users. The relationship between the two organisations – confirmed by the constitutional arrangements adopted under the Fraser Report – was an uneasy one. TRADA's utility to the different parts of the trade varied. To many small and medium sized firms, which could not undertake their own research, it was of importance; larger companies were not so supportive. But all firms, when profits were being squeezed, questioned the necessity of an organisation for which they paid, without immediately apparent benefit. Short-term necessity forced companies to have a short-term outlook. A large number of softwood importers believed that their product was a 'known' quantity not requiring extensive promotion and many shippers already organised their own advertising and marketing. The Association's difficulties were intertwined, therefore, with dual expectations; while conducting scientific research, it was expected by the TTF to publicise and promote the uses of wood. But its ethos remained predominantly one of scientific enquiry rather than salesmanship.[12]

By founding the National Wood Council in 1974, the TTF attempted to meet some of the recommendations in the Fraser Report. The trade was asked to pool its efforts and undertake generic, cooperative advertising, and, with an initially modest budget of £200,000, to join TRADA in presenting practical information to suppliers and consumers. In the following year, it embarked on a policy of consumer advertising, despite the continued opposition of softwood traders and shippers who specified their preference for technical advice and public relations. Many companies did not consider advertising – unlike arbitration, contract forms, and the collating of statistics – to be the task of a trade federation. Within a short time, the Council had overspent its budget, and the TTF's Director General, Sidney Redman, and its President, Heinz Sherwood, asked TRADA to take over the NWC. As a result, the Council ceased its activities in commercial promotion and a Timber Promotion Steering Committee was founded to provide information for architects and designers. Meanwhile, TRADA attempted to counter the growing use of man-made substitutes. In 1975, it established a new public relations team to promote wood as a material that was highly insulating, readily available, low-energy consuming, non-polluting, fire-resistant and, if treated, rot proof. It also assisted companies with training courses, metrication, stress grading, BSI standards, and the provision of technical and educational information. Advertising was limited to a house journal, the supply of materials for exhibitions and information sheets on wood.[13] With more funds from TTF, the Association expanded its role and, in 1976, began to produce a full colour publication entitled *Concept in Wood*, which was distributed free to architects, structural engineers and designers. The journal presented designs and fine examples of woodwork, emphasising both the technical and aesthetic qualities of timber, but it foundered in 1977 due to lack of money. Despite this setback and the indifference shown by parts of the trade to advertising, some hardwood and panel product traders determined to press ahead with a campaign intended to broaden consumer markets. As a result, a National Hardwood Campaign was begun in 1981.

TRADA, in fulfilling its research function, investigated matters such as fire resistance, wood preservation and finishes, timber frame housing and farm buildings, and, as in the case of motorway signs, the uses for panel products. But as the government's support for timber research and development was a declining one, the burden began to lean more heavily on a sceptical industry. The state had once supplied TRADA with some 50 per cent of its income, but the figure gradually declined. From 1973, direct grants to recognised organisations were reduced whilst those for specific projects increased, so that, by 1976, the government provided only 20 per cent of TRADA's financing. The TTF contributed 50 per cent itself, at least half of the Federation's gross income, and the gap of 30 per cent had to be earned. In 1981, TRADA received a sum of £700,000 from the TTF whose overall expenditure was just over £1m.[14] But the services expected in return and the relationship between contributing companies, Federation and Association remained unresolved issues. In the meantime, the government's financial contribution continued to diminish.

The story of timber-frame housing emerged in the 1980s as a prime example of both organisations' inability to adequately respond to adverse media publicity. During the postwar period, significant economies in the use of building timber had been achieved. Pre-cutting before the wood arrived on site had made savings, half of which had been achieved through the pre-fabrication of truss rafters and floorings. Stress grading, by informing builders which standardised piece of timber was exactly appropriate, had encouraged further efficiency. As pre-fabricated parts could be easily delivered ready for use, TRADA decided to promote the timber frame construction of houses, a method of building already common in Scotland and in wood-exporting countries like Canada, Sweden, and Finland. By 1983, timber frame accounted for about 25 per cent of housing starts, but, in June of that year, Thames Television's 'World in Action' ran an edition entitled 'Your Home in Their Hands'. The programme emphasised particular problems with timber frame construction, namely bad site practice, leading to risks of rotting, and fire hazards. TRADA had given warnings about the vital importance of good site practice, but not all builders had heeded the advice. TRADA adopted a low-key response, merely asking builders to seek their guidance or that of the National House Building Consortium. But timber frame construction slumped precipitately, despite the Building Research Establishment refuting wilder allegations and arguing that it was a safe, sound and economical means of construction. By 1986, timber frame starts in England had fallen to about 4 per cent; in Scotland they declined from 47 to 32 per cent in the same period.[15] The trade was slow to appreciate the damage done to the reputation of timber-frame houses, but the controversy eventually had a positive outcome when the Timber and Brick Homes Consortium was founded in 1985 to promote both construction materials jointly.

The tragic fire at the Bradford Football Club stadium, also in 1983, posed further challenges to the defence of wood as a construction material. The TTF and TRADA, in this case, combined to protect timber from adverse publicity. The Federation gave evidence to the ensuing Popplewell Inquiry, and when the report was issued in October 1985, it had toned down initial criticism of timber's contribution to the

SOFTWOOD IMPORTERS MISSION TO CANADA, MARCH 1989

Seaboard International Terminal, North Vancouver, British Columbia

BACK ROW (*left to right*)
Gareth Howe (Snow's Timber); Bob Kerr (Department of Industry, Science and Technology, Canadian Federal Government); Tim Bennett (Bennetts & Co. (Grimsby) Limited); Kevin Hayes (Meyer International PLC); Guy Juneau (Department of External Affairs, Canadian Federal Government); Ronnie Guilford (Heiton McFerran Limited); Ken Chalk (Meon Valley Timber Co. Limited); John Cullingford (Seaboard International Terminal).

FRONT ROW (*left to right*)
Austin Lockyer (The Timber Trade Federation); Peter Hewlett (Nixon Knowles & Co. Limited); Sharon Cork (COFI); Neil Donaldson (James Donaldson & Sons Limited); Hugh Kibblewhite (H & C Timber & Building Supplies Limited).

Pre-fabricated building being moved by crane.
Courtesy of 'Forests Forever'.

disaster. By the time of the King's Cross underground fire in 1987, TRADA had learned from experience and was on the scene promptly to counter the media's immediate conclusion that wooden escalators were wholly to blame.

The debate over TRADA's research role continued throughout these events. In 1986, the TTF's Director General, Austin Lockyer, acknowledged at a trade conference that timber's future in the raw materials market was linked to a strong research and development organisation influenced by the Federation. By this date, the TTF was spending some two-thirds of its income on TRADA. The Association's difficulties were linked to the continued decline of the small, family firm and the growing prominence of larger units which, despite not needing its services as much, contributed most to the TTF's budget. Shippers doubted that they received sufficient benefit from TRADA, and softwood importers thought any research should be conducted not by them but in the timber's country of origin.[16] At the Federation's conference in 1989, TRADA's Director, Dr. C. Gill, tried to convince members that, especially with the European Community introducing common standards and building regulations, a central provider of information on timber products was essential.[17] But many companies wanted the choice of TTF or TRADA membership, so in 1991 it was decided that the institutional links between the two organisations would be broken. While the Association would make available the results of scientific investigation and provide training facilities, the Federation would concentrate on timber promotion, rights to standard contract forms, statistical information, legal, shipping and trade advice, industrial relations expertise, arbitration, and the CBI pension scheme. These were benefits common to many trade associations, but the Diversion Insurance (Timber) Association Ltd. was unique. The scheme had been established by Peter Meyer of Meyer International in 1972 and was open to all importers of timber and panel products. It was introduced as a result of numerous dock strikes, when imports would be diverted to other ports. The insurance scheme covered the importer for additional costs incurred due to industrial action.[18]

III: MARKETING AND ENVIRONMENTALISM, 1979–1992

Clearly, TRADA, with its emphasis on scientific research, could not fulfil the tasks of a marketing organisation, and the TTF's attempt to promote timber through the National Wood Council had not been notably successful. The trade had been complacent, and had concentrated on the sufficiency of timber supplies rather than on expansion of its market share. There were some obvious reasons why this was so. Marketing – in a mass consumer society – was important to all types of business, but it was those businesses engaged in the provision of mass-produced consumer goods that most needed modern marketing techniques and spent most on advertising. Branded, packaged goods like soap and chocolate, durables like cars and washing machines, and personal financial services were made or provided on a large scale and were advertised through the mass media directly to millions. Such businesses also enjoyed returns to scale in production and advertising, and gained oligopolistic advantages over competitors. But, makers and providers of industrial products, selling to a smaller number of customers, did not require such a marketing commitment, and small firms had neither the same needs nor the same resources as large-scale makers of consumer products. Despite the emergence of several larger companies, many firms in the timber trade remained small in scale and, in their sales operations, dependent on a few established contacts rather than on the need to project their wares to millions. In any case, small and medium sized timber importers did not have the funds to support heavy advertising. The TTF could promote timber only as a generic product, for, unlike brick or concrete manufacturers, it had no direct interest in advertising. The Fraser Report had acknowledged the trade's weakness in marketing. Many importers and merchants tended to regard timber as an essential raw material with evident advantages over competing materials, and, to them, its role in the building industry was, likewise, too obvious to need clarification.[19]

Fluctuating trade did not help the cause of marketing: in times of recession, timber firms saw advertising as a tangible, reducable cost and not as an intangible investment. Consequently, promotion did not feature as an item high on TTF agendas in the 1970s, although there were indications of improvement early in the following decade. The larger importers began promoting more forcefully and competitively, but they emphasised their role as providers of timber and did not push specific products. The trade was responding to the problems faced at that time by all those involved in the building industry. By April 1980, it was evident that cuts in local authority expenditure would affect housing starts, and this decision coincided with the deepest economic depression since the War. High interest rates also discouraged the housing and building conversion market. Between 1980 and 1983, the number of houses and flats completed fell from 236,000 to 199,000. Despite signs of some revival between 1984 and 1988, the peak being 229,000, the numbers fell in 1989–90 to 207,000 and 187,000 respectively following the return of another economic slump and high interest rates.[20]

Throughout his term as President of the TTF in the mid-1980s, George Donaldson urged members to meet harsher market circumstances with better salesmanship and improved quality and reliability of product, believing timber companies could better exploit their entrepreneurial opportunities. In effect, the industry had individually and collectively to improve its marketing and so encourage timber consumption. In 1986, the Federation appealed for £250,000 to finance a 'Think Wood' advertising campaign, yet support from member firms, after initial enthusiasm, was disappointing, and, despite the Council of Forest Industries from British Columbia donating £4,000, most overseas shippers failed to contribute. TTF members who did soon became disillusioned with paying for promotions that also benefited rival noncontributors. Economic difficulties put pressure on the profit levels of firms and, therefore, on TTF income, and membership numbers were falling. It was questionable, therefore, if the Federation could sustain its current range of activities.

When he spoke at the 1986 TTF Conference in Birmingham, the Director General, Austin Lockyer, outlined the future of the timber trade, and argued for a stronger, more centralised Federation. He contended that the agents, importers, merchants and international sections within the TTF created artificial barriers in an increasingly integrated business, and he especially wanted more manufacturers and retailers to join. Vertical amalgamations between firms had, as we have seen, continuously undermined divisions between process-stage functions. Commodity-based sections would, perhaps, widen the scope for joint action within the aegis of the TTF. In 1987, hardwood firms finally formed, within the Federation, one National Hardwood Association from the National Hardwood Importers, Agents and Brokers, Merchants and International sections. The softwood trade soon followed, founding a united National Association for Softwood. Both of these new groups were represented on the Federation Council.[21] Financial constraints, however, continued to hinder any new initiatives. The year 1988 was designated 'Timber Promotion Year', but, by 1989 it was decided to scale down the 'Think Wood' campaign. The resignation of the Hunter Timber Group Ltd., part of the multinational Wickes group and one of the Federation's largest members and contributors, seemed to indicate the inherent limitations of joint action. In 1991, the promotional budget of the Federation was halved, although the reinstatement of the 'Think Wood' campaign was planned for 1993.[22]

By the middle of the 1980s, the timber trade faced an additional threat, for which an adequate marketing response was required: a substantial and expanding portion of public opinion began vociferously to question the very ethics of consuming wood. Timber, of course, was not the only product to be criticised. The goals of mass consumption – the pursuit of individual satisfaction and social status through material possessions – began to be queried. Mass consumption itself was a recent phenomenon, occurring after the privations of the Second World War, and offering to most inhabitants of the industrialised, free market economies of the West and Japan, a poverty-free, even quality lifestyle. It met material needs and, emerging as the defining element of these societies and a central part of popular culture, it encountered, in the beginning, very few critics. Nonetheless, some anxiety was expressed at the seemingly unbalanced emphasis upon personal consumption at the expense of 'social' goals such as education, welfare, and the improvement and maintenance of urban and rural environments. Criticism was levelled, furthermore, against the ethics of buying goods from some countries such as South Africa. Attacks were made on the cruelties of the fur trade, and animal welfare and vegetarianism emerged as controversial moral issues.

As a result, marketing theorists started to question long-established principles: while modern marketing still concentrated upon the unlimited satisfaction of

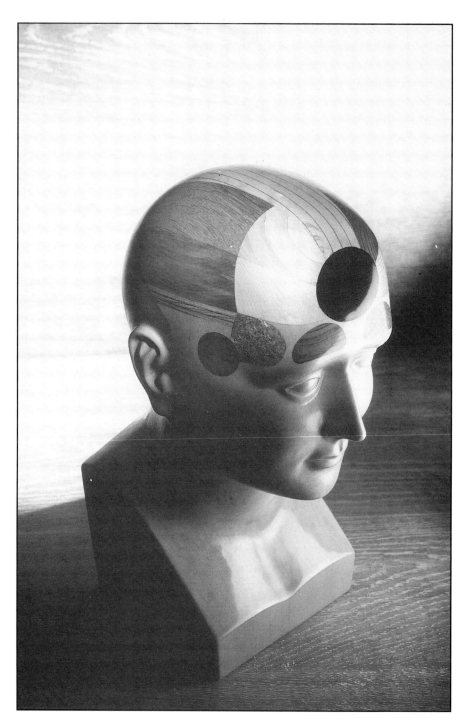

The 'Think Wood' Head.
Courtesy of Travis Dale & Partners, London.

economic, psychological and social desires, the advertising and public relations industries began to recognise widening unease about the morality of particular products, however they might satisfy personal, short-term interests. Sophisticated marketing operations had to take account of 'societal marketing' issues in which the public's changing attitudes and beliefs had to be considered. No company or industry wanted to be the centre of general controversy or opprobrium, for, even if they did not share public concern, clearly bad publicity was commercially disadvantageous. Companies were becoming conscious of looming controversy over the environmental impact of unlimited and unregulated production. If the majority of the public was not diverted from the pleasures of mass consumption, demands for the responsible use of finite resources and for curbs on pollution did have a direct impact on many industries.[23] In the 1980s, the timber industry became a target for the environmentalist movement. The destruction of undeveloped lands and natural forest habitats in the tropics of South America, East Asia, and Africa attracted the fiercest criticism. Pictures of burnt-out tropical rain forests on the television were visible to all and became associated in the minds of the public with the timber trade. Worldwide and local opposition also arose against logging in Canada and the United States, and even Scandinavia and Scotland were highlighted, because, although these countries' forests were self-sustaining, replanting was changing natural landscapes and environments. In addition, the chemical processing of wood for pulp and paper raised problems of pollution. How the timber trade responded to these ecological issues was to become crucial to the public's continued faith in wood as a plentiful and responsibly exploited commodity.

The World Wildlife Fund led general unease about the depletion of forests. Unsustainable felling, the ruination of natural habitats, and the invasion and exploitation of Indian territories – especially in the Amazon basin – were specific areas of controversy. The timber trade felt unfairly attacked, but it was not always quick to respond, and when the WWF was joined by the even more critical Friends of the Earth, the National Hardwood Importers Section of the TTF demanded an effective reply. Figures from the United Nations' Food and Agriculture Organisation showed that some 70 per cent of all forest clearance was undertaken not for timber exports, but for food production, ranching, and local fuel and timber needs. Seeking to counter the claims of environmentalist pressure groups, the TTF's President, E.M.L. Latham, agreed to speak at an FoE conference. The Hardwood Section followed this initiative by meeting the FoE, and urged it to campaign against the worst excesses of felling and not against British imports. Such a step was a departure from the timber trade's traditional stance, the view that forest management was the responsibility of the supplying country. In 1985, a public relations executive had been recruited by the TTF, and an 'Ecological Sub-Committee' was formed to argue the industry's case, namely that the management of tropical forests on a sustainable basis was dependent upon the cooperation of exporters, importers, environmentalists, indigenous populations and governments.

The Federation had supported the International Tropical Timber Agreement, signed by the United Kingdom and 40 other countries in 1984, and the Tropical Forests Action Programme as set out by the United Nations' Food and Agricultural Organisation in 1985. An International Tropical Timber Organisation was founded in 1987 at Yokohama, Japan, and it was charged with creating a frame-work for cooperation between exporting and consuming countries. Arguing that international trade should benefit all participants, the ITTO defended the right of producers to receive better remuneration, and urged the relocation of processing facilities in supply countries. Its aims included improved forest management, distribution and market-ing, and it sought to encourage production policies based upon sustainable utilisation, conservation and ecological balance. Through the TFAP, donor governments, such as that of the UK, provided funding for the development and conservation of tropical forest resources.[24]

The President of the TTF, George Donaldson, continued throughout 1986 to exhort members, arguing that they had to protect their market and counter the accusations of environmentalists. In its crusade to protect the trade's commercial interests, the Federation campaigned by way of press releases, letters to newspapers, meetings with government ministers, and the provision of speakers. When, in 1988, the FoE picketed a number of retailers and published a *Good Wood Guide* for consumers and a *Good Wood Manual* for architects and manufacturers, relationships with the environmentalists reach their nadir, and the hardwood section ceased all contact and talks. News that many local authorities, architects and purchase managers were deliberately proscribing wood forced the timber trade to recognise one factor: it needed to increase its influence within producer countries and so curb unsustainable felling and ecological damage.[25]

In May 1990, the ITTO announced its goal of achieving 'sustainable tropical forest management' by the year 2000. The World Wide Fund for Nature – the renamed World Wildlife Fund – was broadly supportive, although it had already set 1995 as its target year. As well as highlighting the catastrophes of the Amazon and East Asia, the WWF was critical of poor practice in Canada, Chile and the Soviet Union. The Canadians adopted a national strategy for conservation and development, but virgin forest area continued to decline, and, in British Columbia, diverging economic and environmental interests produced an intense political debate. In the United States, it was undoubtedly true that planting more than matched the rate of logging but irreplaceable trees and habitats continued to be lost. The giant redwoods of the Southwest Coast were threatened, and fears that the northern spotted owl's survival was endangered turned public opinion in the states of Oregon and Washington against lumber firms, despite concern about job losses.[26] Information from the ITTO demonstrated an alarming annual rate of destruction in Malaysia, Indonesia and Borneo, and it noted the virtual extinction of virgin forest in Thailand and the Philippines. Reports of understaffed forestry departments and conservation bodies, illegal logging, the evasion of reforestation levies, and disregard for sustainable quotas also raised fears.[27]

Four areas following 'sustainable' forest logging practices. 1. Dipterocarp forest in Indonesia recently logged.
Courtesy of the Council of Forest Industries, British Columbia, American Hardwood Export Council and 'Forests Forever'.

2. Canadian plantation forest.

(*Opposite*) 3. North American temperate forest.

4. Log booms floating down river to a mill in Canada.

In November, 1989, the TTF, the British Woodworking Federation, the British Furniture Manufacturers Federation, numerous embassies and high commissions, home grown producers, and the pulp and paper industry combined to consider the raising of £400,000 for the 'Forests Forever' campaign. Its object was to inform the British public of the importance and role of forests and wood products. T.S. Mallinson, the TTF President, was appointed in 1990 to head the Campaign. The TTF had, at that time, both a Promotion and an Environment Committee, the functions of each being seen as separate. It was decided to combine the two committees and appoint a public relations executive, Michael James, a former diplomat, to refute criticism of timber consumption and direct the 'Forests Forever' Campaign. With the United Kingdom still importing some 80 per cent of its needs, consumers were to be made aware of their dependency on imports, and foreign suppliers of their responsibility for good forest management. The UK timber trade believed that its members were behaving far more responsibly than those in Japan and most of Europe, and that it was the duty of the TTF and the 'Forests Forever' Campaign to raise the public awareness. The TTF's Environment and Promotion Committee found that most of its public relations programme revolved around environmental issues in any case and the FFC produced a considerable amount of further material. A *Real Wood Guide*, for example, illustrated the availability of world resources, and demonstrated how sustainable and environmentally friendly forests, both temperate and tropical, might be managed.

The need for action was highlighted by a United Nations' Report in 1991: it showed 17m hectares of tropical rainforest disappearing every year. The 'Forests Forever' Campaign then sought the support of the WWF for environmental policies that could

Forests Forever logo

be voluntarily adopted by all UK companies, whether traders or end users, and a joint accord was agreed in September, 1991. Its ultimate aim was to ensure that timber would not be internationally traded unless it was obtained from an environmentally-sound source. It was agreed that timber supplies would be labelled after independent verification and checking of sources of supply. This wood and wood product purchasing policy encompassed the ITTO's programme for sustainable management of tropical forests by the year 2000, although the WWF continued to favour 1995. These policies were then extended to the exploitation of temperate forests, including those in the UK. In effect, the British timber trade was using its commercial relationships with producers to influence their forest management. There were still questions, notably from the Friends of the Earth, about a scheme reliant on producers with challengeable credibility. In the Amazon, clearances by ranchers, farmers, mining companies and locals were seemingly unaffected, and still attracted the protests of environmentalists. But the 'Forests Forever' Campaign did express the British timber trade's genuine wish to be associated with environmentally appropriate material, and, of course, its long-term future depended on sustainability. Timber's commercial viability rested on the trade meeting public concerns, and there was no benefit to be gained from the exhausting of supplies.[28]

What impact might these policy developments have on the British timber industry? As we have seen, the declining application and use of wood in the post-war period and rapidly rising prices had been capped by problems in the 1980s housing market. As a result, the real value of the timber trade, despite frequent fluctuations, had remained fairly static throughout the 1950s and 1960s, but experienced, as did its percentage of the UK import bill, a decline in the 1970s and 1980s. Consumption per head fell – to approximately the levels of 100 years before – as growing consumer incomes were spent elsewhere. In short, the British timber trade had since the Second World War faced a declining market, and it needed to improve its marketing to user firms and the public if this trend was to be reversed. Quite simply, its customers could buy alternatives to wood, and the case for timber – its utility, naturalness and consumer appeal – had to be vigorously demonstrated. But, latterly, it had to prove to a growing section of the population that wood was both environmentally and commercially, viable.

So long as the campaign for sustainability could be won in producing countries, the planting of trees to provide timber – a natural, organic resource – was clearly advantageous, and the processing of this commodity could be shown to be less polluting and energy-hungry than man-made substitutes. If it could not prove its case, the timber trade might be permanently damaged. While the controversy was concentrated upon tropical hardwoods – but by no means exclusively – it did reflect on the whole trade and its legitimacy. The need for the commodity had previously been accepted, despite the development of man-made substitutes, and the TTF, as we have seen, had campaigned for due recognition of its trade in the formulation of economic, commercial and transport policy. The new situation demanded some form of collective action: the Federation and the 'Forests Forever' Campaign were endeavouring to exercise maximum influence over suppliers and the support of member firms was crucial. A marketing and public information initiative, highlighting the Campaign and arguing the case for timber was also required. But commitment to collective action within a varied and differentiated trade was far from universal. Perhaps there was one lesson from history: the methods and trade structure established in the pre-war and inter-war periods had suited the market circumstances of their time, but they needed to be altered if new organisational, marketing and environmental imperatives were to be met.

REFERENCES

1. Foreman-Peck, 1983, pp.370–85; Van der Wee, 1991, pp.380–420, 479–523.

2. Ibid.

3. *The Times*, 21 Feb 1974, Timber Supplement, p.23.

4. Ibid.; Interview with L.A. Woodburn-Bamberger, 10 Oct 1991.

5. *The Times*, 14 Feb 1975, p.26.

6. *Financial Times*, 5 March 1975, Timber Supplement.

7. *Report of the Commission of Inquiry into Industrial and Commercial Representation*, 1972, pp.30, 63.

8. Fraser, *Report . . .*, 1973, p.1; TTF Council Minutes, 14 & 17 Oct 1973; Interview with L.A. Woodburn-Bamberger.

9. W. Grant & D. Marsh, *The CBI*, 1977, pp.137–217.

10. *The Times*, 21 Feb 1974, Timber Supplement; *Financial Times*, 30 Nov 1991, p.XIV.

11. Central Office of Information, Reference Services, *Forestry in Britain*, 1989.

12. B. Latham, 'The Story of the T.D.A. and T.R.A.D.A., 1934–74', pp.2–5; Interviews with J.G. Sunley, 3 Oct 1991, G.A. Donaldson, 3 Oct 1991, T.S. Mallinson, 3 Oct 1991.

13. *Bulletin*, Dec 1974, Annex B.

14. TTF Council Minutes, 14 Oct 1981.

15. TTF Statistics.

16. A.A. Lockyer, TTF Director-General, 'The Way Ahead for the Timber Trade Federation', TTF Conference, 1986.

17. C. Gill, 'The Role of a Research and Development Association and the Support it Needs from the Trade', TTF Conference, 1989.

18. Interview with P.B. Meyer, 6 Nov 1991; Lockyer, 'The Way Ahead . . .', 1986.

19. Fraser, *Report . . .*, pp.5–6.

20. Mitchell, 1990.

21. TTF Executive Committee Minutes, 15 Apr 1987.

22. Interview with D.P.R. Morgan, 26 Mar 1992.

23. Cf. Sheth & Garret, *Marketing Theory: Evolution and Evaluation*, 1985; J.K. Galbraith, *The Affluent Society*, 1958.

24. World Wide Fund for Nature, 'Tropical Forests Update', Jan 1991.

25. TTF Executive Committee, 30 Nov 1988.

26. World Wide Fund for Nature, 'Why 1995?', 1991; *The Economist*, 26 May 1990, p.78; 22 June 1991; *Financial Times*, 2 Jan 1991, p.26.

27. Ibid.; *The Economist*, 26 May 1990, p.78.

28. Ibid.; *Forests Forever*, Briefing Paper, Feb 1991; *Victoria Times-Colonist*, 9 Sept 1991, p.A9; *Financial Times*, 30 Oct 1991, p.20; Interview with D.P.R. Morgan, 26 Mar 1992.

APPENDICES

I: PRESIDENTS OF
THE TIMBER TRADE FEDERATION

1893–97	Sir Samuel B. Boulton, Bt., *Burt, Boulton & Haywood Ltd., London*
1897–99	Alderman C.H. Low, *Taylor & Low Bros. Ltd., Bristol*
1899–1901	J.H. Fisher, JP, *Tealby & Co. Ltd., Hull*
1901–3	T.F.C. May, *May & Hassell Ltd., London and Bristol*
1903–6	C.J. Morgan, *Foy Morgan & Co. Ltd., London*
1906–8	A. Dobell, *Alfred Dobell & Co. Ltd., Liverpool*
1908–10	A. Farquharson, *Farquharson Timber Ltd., London*
1910–11	Sir John Fleming, DL, JP, *John Fleming & Co. Ltd., Aberdeen*
1911–12	R.F. Springhall, JP, *R.F. Springhall & Sons Ltd., Kings Lynn*
1912–14	G.H. Lindsey-Renton, *G.H. Renton & Co. Ltd., London*
1914–16	J. Gallatly, *John Gallatly & Son, London*
1916–19	L. Bamberger, *Bambergers Ltd., London*
1919–20	R. Jewson, JP, *Jewson & Sons Ltd., Norwich*
1920–3	H.E. Knott, OBE, JP, *Marshall, Knott & Barker Ltd., Grimsby*
1923–6	E. Locks Latham, *James Latham Ltd., London*
1926–8	C. Gane, JP, *Charles Gane & Co. Ltd., London*
1928–9	H.C. David, JP, *Robinson, David & Co. Ltd., Cardiff*
1929–31	E.P. Tetsall, *Wm. Brown & Co. (Ipswich) Ltd., Ipswich*
1931–3	E.C. Horton, OBE, *B. Horton & Son Ltd., Westerham, Kent*
1933–4	E.W.H. Beaton, *Tagart, Beaton & Co., London*
1934–6	P.B. Meyer, *Montague L. Meyer Ltd., London*
1936–7	Sir Edward B. Monkhouse, CBE, *Duncan, Ewing & Co. Ltd., Liverpool*
1937–9	Sir Archibald Harris, *Bambergers Ltd., London*
1939	W.O. Woodward, *The Nottingham Mills Co. Ltd., Nottingham*
1939–42	L. Arnott, *Pharaoh Gane & Co. Ltd., London*, Acting President (1939–40), President (1940–2)
1942–5	J.L. Baynes, CBE, *Gabriel, Wade & English Ltd., London*
1945–7	B. Latham, CBE, MM, MA, *James Latham Ltd., London*
1947–9	Major W. Newland Hillas, *W.N. Hillas & Co. Ltd., Hull*
1949–51	N.A. Wright, *C. Leary & Co., London*
1951–2	H.R. Woodburn-Bamberger, *Bambergers Ltd., London*
1952–4	T.A. Storey, *Williams Evans & Co. (Manchester) Ltd., Widnes, Lancs.*
1954–5	F. Urmston, *Hallam Ramsay & Co. Ltd., London*
1955–7	L.A. Bayman, *George E. Gray Ltd., Ilford*
1957–9	J.S. Gordon Clark, *Churchill & Sim Ltd., London*
1959–61	W.E. Vesey, MBE, FCA, *Christie & Vesey Ltd., London*
1961–3	P.B. Meyer, *Montague L. Meyer Ltd., London*

1963–5	B.B. Kennedy, *James Kennedy & Co. Ltd., Glagow*
1965–7	L.H. Storey, FCA, *William Evans & Co. (Manchester) Ltd., Widnes, Lancs.*
1967–9	P. Morgan, *Price & Pierce (Holding Co.) Ltd., London*
1969–71	R.E. Groves, CBE, *J. Gliksten & Son Ltd., London*
1971–3	A.D.C. Smith, *Horsley Smith & Jewson Ltd., Hull*
1973–5	L.A. Woodburn-Bamberger, *Bambergers (Timber & Plywood) Ltd., London*
1975–7	H. Sherwood, *Parker Timber Co. Ltd., London*
1977–9	J.I. Gammie, MC, *Sabah Timber Co. Ltd., London*
1979–81	R.S. Howard, *W.W. Howard Bros. (Investments) Ltd., London*
1981–2	C.S. Cotterell, *Machin & Kingsley Ltd., London*
1982–4	M.E. Brown, *Meyer International PLC, London*
1984–5	E.M.L. Latham, *James Latham PLC, London*
1985–7	G.N. Donaldson, *James Donaldson & Sons Ltd., Leven*
1987–9	C.R. Carr, TD, *Sandell Perkins PLC, Maidstone*
1989–91	T.S. Mallinson, *Mallinson-Denny Limited*
1991–	L.C.L. Groth, *Stora Timber AB*

II: DIRECTORS GENERAL OF THE TIMBER TRADE FEDERATION

S. Redman, CB   1973–82

L.A. Woodburn-Bamberger   1982–5

A.A. Lockyer, LVO   1985–92

P.G. Harris   1992–

President 1982–4 M.E. Brown

President 1984–5 E.M.L. Latham

President 1985–7 G.N. Donaldson

President 1987–9 C.R. Carr

President 1989–91 T.S. Mallison

President 1991–   L.C.L. Groth

III: TIMBER TRADE STATISTICS
TIMBER IMPORTS TO THE UNITED
KINGDOM, 1870–1985

Date	Volume millions m³	£m (cif) Current Values	% of UK Import	Wholesale Price Index (1890 = 100)	£m Constant Values
1870		13.1	4.3	—	—
1871	5.9	12.1	3.7	150.4	8.0
1872		13.8	3.9	154.1	9.0
1873		18.8	5.1	166.4	11.3
1874		22.0	5.9	170.0	12.9
1875		15.4	4.1	148.5	10.4
1876		19.1	5.1	150.4	12.7
1877		20.3	5.1	146.7	13.8
1878		14.0	3.8	128.3	10.9
1879		10.8	3.0	111.7	9.7
1880		16.7	4.1	127.0	13.1
1881	8.3	14.6	3.7	128.3	11.4
1882		16.8	4.1	131.4	12.8
1883		16.7	3.9	127.0	13.1
1884		14.5	3.7	112.9	12.8
1885		14.8	4.0	104.2	14.2
1886		12.2	3.5	97.5	12.5
1887		11.7	3.2	91.5	12.8
1888		14.3	3.7	97.5	14.7
1889		19.5	4.6	108.6	18.0
1890		16.7	4.0	100.0	16.7
1891	9.4	15.6	3.6	92.1	16.9
1892		17.8	4.2	92.1	19.3
1893		16.1	4.0	85.9	18.7
1894		17.8	4.4	82.2	21.7
1895		16.4	3.9	83.5	19.6
1896		20.3	4.6	88.1	23.0
1897		24.6	5.5	88.4	27.8
1898		22.1	4.7	90.1	24.5
1899		24.2	5.0	89.0	27.2

1900		27.9	5.3	94.5	29.5
1901	13.4	24.6	4.7	89.6	27.5
1902		25.2	4.8	84.1	30.0
1903		27.1	5.0	85.9	31.5
1904		23.7	4.3	81.0	29.3
1905		23.3	4.1	82.9	28.1
1906		27.5	4.5	84.7	32.5
1907		27.1	4.2	87.1	31.1
1908		24.3	4.1	82.9	29.3
1909		23.6	3.8	79.2	29.8
1910		26.2	3.9	79.8	32.8
1911	13.7	25.9	3.8	83.5	31.0
1912		28.4	3.8	93.3	30.4
1913	16.4	33.8	4.4	90.3	37.4
1914		25.3	3.6	93.3	27.1
1915		32.8	3.9	134.4	24.4
1916		40.2	4.2	202.6	19.8
1917		25.6	2.4	270.8	9.5
1918		29.2	2.2	333.0	8.8
1919		72.3	4.4	326.0	22.2
1920		82.1	4.2	336.0	24.4
1921	6.8(a)	30.0(a)	2.8	198.6	15.1
1922(b)	12.5	37.3	3.7	143.0	26.1
1923	14.6	47.7	4.4	148.9	32.0
1924	16.4	51.1	4.0	143.1	35.7
1925	16.1	46.5	3.5	121.7	38.2
1926	13.1	40.9	3.3	125.7	32.5
1927	18.0	51.3	4.2	125.2	41.0
1928	14.7	44.7	3.7	125.6	35.6
1929	16.3	48.8	4.0	121.7	40.1
1930	14.5	45.3	4.3	118.8	38.1
1931	12.2	31.2	3.6	98.5	31.7
1932	12.6	27.8	3.9	81.4	34.2
1933	13.8	31.7	4.7	89.6	35.4
1934	16.3	42.2	5.8	100.1	42.2
1935	16.2	39.0	5.2	110.7	35.2
1936	16.2	47.6	5.6	120.1	39.6
1937	16.2	66.7	6.5	111.9	59.6
1938	12.2	46.2	5.0	89.4	51.7
1939	10.3	39.8	4.5	79.4	50.1

1940	5.7	40.5	3.6	145.6	27.8
1941	3.2	26.7	2.3	189.2	14.1
1942	2.4	22.1	1.8	224.6	9.8
1943	3.3	38.3	2.0	288.7	13.3
1944	3.5	43.6	1.8	332.4	13.1
1945	5.1	52.7	3.5	319.9	16.5
1946	5.2	62.0	3.4	319.2	19.4
1947	9.1	125.8	7.0	392.6	32.0
1948	7.1	101.8	4.9	470.8	21.6
1949	7.6	109.1	4.8	480.7	22.7
1950	6.8	101.4	3.9	507.5	20.0
1951	10.9	237.5	6.1	655.3	36.2
1952	7.3	178.0	5.1	720.8	24.6
1953	9.2	173.6	5.2	653.3	26.6
1954	9.2	179.8	5.4	681.2	26.4
1955	10.6	224.7	5.8	724.8	31.0
1956	8.5	181.4	4.7	717.3	25.3
1957	8.8	199.3	4.9	720.7	27.7
1958	8.1	167.0	4.5	690.7	24.2
1959	9.7	169.2	4.2	651.2	26.0
1960	12.0	219.8	4.8	710.5	30.9
1961	10.9	208.0	4.7	723.4	28.8
1962	10.4	193.0	4.3	701.8	27.5
1963	11.0	207.1	4.3	734.3	28.2
1964	12.9	262.3	4.8	760.9	34.5
1965	12.4	267.2	4.6	807.2	33.1
1966	10.8	240.2	4.0	805.2	29.8
1967	11.1	253.5	3.9	802.5	31.6
1968	11.8	302.5	3.8	893.7	33.8
1969	10.4	284.0	3.1	1190.5	23.9
1970	11.2	320.2	3.5	1247.6	25.7
1971	12.2	332.0	3.4	1299.4	25.6
1972	12.8	366.0	3.3	1391.7	26.3
1973	15.8	646.7	4.1	2441.6	26.5
1974	12.7	753.3	3.3	3227.3	23.3
1975	9.1	539.1	2.2	2974.2	18.1
1976	11.4	808.8	2.6	3918.2	20.6
1977	10.3	868.6	2.4	4738.7	18.3
1978	11.0	906.6	2.3	4398.3	20.6
1979	12.1	1110.0	2.7	5012.8	22.1
1980	9.8	968.5	2.1	5689.9	17.0

1981	9.3	968.1	2.1	5610.3	17.3
1982	9.9	1022.3	2.0	5593.2	18.3
1983	11.8	1394.7	2.4	6406.8	21.8
1984	11.3	1497.1	2.1	7300.2	20.5
1985	9.2	1406.7	1.9	7704.2	18.3

Figures are normally based upon Board of Trade Returns. Volume totals may also vary according to weight-volume conversion ratios selected for particular types of timber import. The classification of so many different import types also creates problems. The most notable example is plywood, included in the above figures, since it is sometimes designated a manufactured item and so not included in commodity import totals. Classification conventions, moreover, have a direct impact on the weights in the wholesale price index, which, in drawing from a variety of sources, is spliced at appropriate points.

(a) figures after 1921 may vary with other published sources because of the inclusion of plywood, sometimes treated separately as a manufactured item.

(b) figures after 1922 do not include the Irish Republic.

Sources: Board of Trade Returns; W. Page, *Commerce and Industry*, 1919; 'Wholesale Prices of Commodities in 1921', *Royal Statistical Society Journal*, vol.lxxxv, 1922, p.292; B.R. Mitchell, *British Historical Statistics*, 1990; Timber Trade Federation, *UK Year Book of Timber Statistics, 1983–85*, 1987; Central Statistical Office.

IV: TIMBER TRADE STATISTICS
TIMBER IMPORTS PER CAPITA TO
THE UNITED KINGDOM, 1871–1981

Date	Imports m cu³	Population millions	Imports per capita cu³
1871	5.9	31.6	0.19
1881	8.3	34.9	0.24
1891	9.4	37.8	0.25
1901	13.4	41.5	0.32
1911	13.7	45.3	0.30
1921	6.8	47.2	0.14
1926	13.1	45.2(a)	0.29
1931	12.2	46.1	0.26
1936	16.2	47.1	0.34
1941	3.2	48.2	0.07
1951	10.9	50.3	0.22
1961	10.9	52.8	0.21
1971	12.2	55.9	0.22
1981	9.3	56.3	0.17

(a) the apparent fall in population is caused by the secession of the Irish Republic.

Sources: Board of Trade Returns; W. Page, *Commerce and Industry*, 1919; B.R. Mitchell, *British Historical Statistics*, 1990; Timber Trade Federation, *UK Year Book of Timber Statistics, 1983–85*, 1987.

V: TIMBER TRADE STATISTICS TIMBER IMPORTS TO THE UNITED KINGDOM BY PERCENTAGE OF COMMODITY, 1920–1980

By Value:

	1921	1930	1940	1950	1960	1970	1980
Softwood	55.5	56.1	59.2	56.3	56.6	53.0	51.7
Hardwood	17.9	19.2	15.6	14.8	14.3	11.1	10.3
Plywood	—	0.1	6.7	7.0	9.3	15.4	9.7
Pitwood	10.6	11.3	11.2	10.6	1.8	—	—
Staves	4.7	1.5	—	—	—	—	—
Sleepers	11.0	5.3	—	—	—	—	—

By Volume:

	1921	1930	1940	1950	1960	1970	1980
Softwood	50.0	58.6	45.5	43.1	70.8	65.8	61.2
Hardwood	5.9	7.6	9.0	29.4	11.7	8.9	7.1
Plywood	—	—	1.1	7.5	5.0	9.8	8.1
Pitwood	26.5	26.9	27.3	7.3	—	—	—
Staves	10.3	6.9	—	—	—	—	—
Sleepers	7.4	5.6	—	3.0	—	—	—

Figures are not shown if less than 0.05 per cent of the import total.

Sources: Board of Trade Returns; Timber Trade Federation, *UK Year Book of Timber Statistics, 1983–85*, 1987.

VI: TIMBER TRADE STATISTICS WORLD EXPORTS AND IMPORTS OF TIMBER, 1960–1980. PERCENTAGE BY COUNTRY BY VALUE (US DOLLARS)

Exports:

	1960	1970	1980
Canada	25.5	21.9	18.8
Finland	12.0	9.7	9.8
France	3.2	2.4	2.6
FR Germany	2.4	2.5	4.2
Italy	0.9	1.2	1.2
Japan	2.6	1.8	1.6
Netherlands	1.6	1.2	1.7
Norway	3.0	2.4	1.7
Sweden	13.8	12.3	10.1
UK	2.1	1.2	1.5
USA	8.0	12.9	12.6
USSR	4.1	6.7	12.6

Imports:

	1960	1970	1980
Canada	2.4	1.1	1.3
Finland	0.2	0.4	0.4
France	3.8	5.7	5.7
FR Germany	9.8	9.4	10.3
Italy	4.8	5.3	6.4
Japan	3.0	13.3	15.5
Netherlands	4.3	4.2	4.3
Norway	0.7	1.1	0.9
Sweden	0.8	0.8	1.1
UK	18.7	12.1	9.4
USA	22.9	16.3	12.3
USSR	1.0	1.4	1.4

Sources: Food and Agricultural Organisation, *Yearbook of Forest Products Statistics*, 1961, & *Yearbook of Forest Statistics, 1970–81*, 1983.

VII: TIMBER TRADE STATISTICS
TIMBER-USING INDUSTRIES OF THE
UNITED KINGDOM, 1907–1970

Date	Gross Output £m	Employees 1000s
1907	33.5	176.0
1924	82.3	189.8
1930	99.8	241.0
1935	112.5	273.3
1949	336.0	285.5
1951	417.3	285.1
1956	480.0	267.6
1963	679.3	262.8
1968	1062.4	257.7
1970	1328.7	267.0

Sources: Business Statistics Office, *Historical Record of the Census of Production, 1907–1970*.

VIII: EVOLUTION OF THE ORGANISATION OF THE TIMBER TRADE FEDERATION

When the Timber Trade Federation was inaugurated in 1892, it was very much a 'federation' of Area Associations consisting of many small family firms. Importers were located near to ports dotted around the UK, and local autonomy was maintained by the TTF focussing mainly on the issues of common interest. In general, businesses within the trade were divided amongst agents, importers and merchants, with the National Softwood Importers being the most important group. Initially, the Federation was comprised of separate committees such as Foreign Timber Importers, Merchants (Foreign and English Timber), Brokers and Agents. An Executive Committee composed of representatives of various branches and local associations, and an elected President provided overall administrative control and took care of the day-to-day running of the TTF. The Merchant Freighters' Association, formed in 1895, dealt with claims by or against freighters or shippers, whilst other important matters such as charter parties, contract forms and arbitration were organised by the Federation.

At the outbreak of World War One, membership had grown from 248 (in 1893) to 629. Sections for merchants, importers, agents and brokers still had liberty of action except in matters affecting the trade as a whole, which were the responsibility of the Executive Committee. This committee was formed from representatives of British timber, hardwood, softwood, London, Scottish and sleeper importer sections along with various Area Associations and English timber merchants. In 1918, it had 67 policy forming members.

Government control of the trade during World War One (*see* Chapter II) was effected with the cooperation of the TTF, but gradual changes occurred and new sections were formed during the inter-war years. An insurance society, The Timber Trade Mutual Fire Insurance Society Ltd., was formed in 1918. The British Timber Section (originally the English Timber Section) changed its name to The Federated Home Grown Timber Merchants Association in 1919. The Federation reorganised in 1920, changing the name of the Executive Committee to the Timber Trade Federation Council. Membership consisted of:

Ex-presidents and ex-vice-presidents (ex-officio members)
Merchants' Section – 5
Federated Home Grown Timber Merchants' Association – 10
Pitwood Importers' Section – 3
Hardwood Section – 6
London Importers' (softwoods) Section – 5
Agents & Brokers' Section – 3

N.E. Coast Section – 2
Western Counties Timber Trade Association – 1
East Anglian & South Lincolnshire Section – 3
Liverpool – 4
Humber District – 7
Bristol Channel – 7
Manchester – 2
Ireland – 2
Scottish Section – 6

A Plywood Section, open to merchants, importers, agents and brokers was formed in 1923, reflecting the growing importance of plywood. The need for a research body resulted in the formation of the Timber Development Association, Ltd. (TDA) in 1934. Other new bodies, such as the Hardwood Agents & Brokers and the Hardwood Importers' Section, were formed in the second half of the 1930's.

When the Second World War started in 1939, the TTF was still very much a decentralised organisation in which the national executive body (Executive Council) recognised the autonomy of the constituent associations, that is, primary loyalty to local associations led to general loyalty to the Federation. As for the timber trade, strict 'discipline' prevailed, with business being done in the traditional way through a chain of shipper, agent/broker, importer, and merchant or large consumer. 'Lists' of members with whom business could be conducted were strictly applied.

During the period of economic controls between 1939 and 1954, closer links were established between the TDA and the TTF. The former's funding was guaranteed and the Executive Council was allowed to nominate 22 of the Association's 30 member Council. A National Veneer Section and the Wallboard Merchants' Association (separate but under the auspices of the TTF) were formed in 1944, and the Sawmilling and Woodworking Section changed its name to the National Sawmilling Association in 1946. The NSA was represented on the Executive Council by its Chairman and five others. By 1950, the list of TTF national sections and associations was as follows:

National Hardwood Importers
National Softwood Importers
National Veneer Section
Merchants' Section
Plywood Section
National Sawmilling Association
Timber Development Association

The increasing complexity of the TTF could be seen at the time of the Monopolies Commission Report in 1953 (Diagram, Chapter IV). Compliance with the strictures of the Report required the abolition of importers' 'lists', the ending of old rigidities and the right of manufacturers to buy timber directly from the shipper without using an agent. As the trade was rationalised in the 1960s, shippers began to set up their own sales offices and the agents, traditionally grouped together in The City, began to move out of London.

Not all of the changes recommended by the Emmerson Report of 1960 were implemented. Those that were included the appointment of the first salaried chairman, Sir John Simpson, in 1961; the formation of a London Association; and a new Executive Committee. During the same year, the new Particle Board Section was established. The growing importance of research was reflected in 1962 by the evolution of the Timber Development Association into the Timber Research and Development Association (TRADA). It worked in partnership with the government's Department of Scientific and Industrial Research.

When Sir Bruce Fraser was called upon some 13 years after Sir Harold Emmerson to study the structure of the TTF, he found the historical demarcations still present within the timber trade. Membership in the Federation was not direct but through national and area organisations. This did not reflect changing conditions in which Area Associations were less important than previously. Firms were becoming bigger and small ports less significant (*see* Chapter V) and, in addition, the new International Section, formed in 1972 of agents and importers, was the fastest growing section. During the 1970s, emphasis throughout the trade shifted to commodity sections.

Although the recommendations of the Fraser Report were designed to further centralise and streamline the TTF, the federal structure remained. Membership did become direct but firms were placed on one of three registers: agents, importers or merchants. Although it was not obligatory for agents and members of the International Division to join Area Associations, merchants and importers were required to do so. The Area Associations made no financial contribution to the TTF, thus losing influence, although they were still directly represented on the TTF Council, which remained in existence. Funding was obtained through subscription and contribution (a levy based on the previous year's trading of member firms). A Director General was appointed, Mr. Sydney Redman, CB, in 1973 and given an Executive Assistant. A President's Advisory Board was constituted and various committees, as well as the Executive Committee, dealt with such matters as investment and legal protection. The TTF began publishing, in 1974, *The Bulletin*, to keep members more fully informed of any matters of concern to the timber trade. The structure of the Federation following the Fraser Report became:

DIVISIONS – 5
    Importers
    Merchants
    Agents
    International
    National Sawmilling Association

SECTIONS – 10
    National Softwood Importers Section
    Softwood Agents and Brokers Section
    Plywood Importers Section
    Plywood Agents and Brokers Section
    National Hardwood Importers Section
    Hardwood Agents and Brokers Section
    Particle Board Importers Section
    Particle Board Agents and Brokers Section
    National Veneer Section
    Sleeper and Pole Section

The Executive Committee was slimmed down in 1983 to include the officers and immediate past President of the TTF plus representatives of the various divisions and sections, TRADA and the largest timber companies. It was the principal initiator of policy, the TTF Council acting more or less as a rubber stamp. In 1990, a further step was taken towards more efficient management: the TTF was incorporated and the Executive Committee was replaced with a smaller Board of Management.

The structure of the TTF had also changed by 1991. Commodity Associations (each composed of agents, merchants and importers) had been formed during the previous decade: namely the National Panel Products Association (1982), the National Hardwood Association (1987) and the National Association for Softwood (1988). The merchants and importers divisions merged in 1991 leaving three divisions: agents, importers/merchants and international. In addition, there was the National Sawmilling Association and the Timber Trade Training Association.

A decision taken in 1991 led to the division of the TTF and TRADA. Membership for each became separate, leaving the TTF relieved of a financial burden that had been its largest outgoing expenditure.

Promotion and environmental matters appear to be key areas of activity in the 1990s. The 'Forests Forever' Campaign, a joint trade/TTF venture, reflects this new emphasis and commercial and marketing requirement.

IX: STRUCTURE OF THE TIMBER TRADE FEDERATION

BOARD OF MANAGEMENT

National Association for Softwood	**National Hardwood Association**	**National Panel Products Association**
Importers/Merchants Division	Importers/Merchants Division	Importers/Merchants Division
NSIS	NHIS	PPIS
Agents Division	Agents Division	Agents Division
SABS	HABS	PPABS
International Division	International Division	International Division

All TTF Members are automatically members of Timber Trade Training Association
Some Members choose to be Members of the National Sawmilling Association
Some Members choose to be Members of the Sleeper & Pole Section

Other Committees

Documentary Committee
Environment & Promotion Committee
Joint Committee re Softwood Statistics
Legal Protection Committee

NSIS – National Softwood Importers Section
NHIS – National Hardwood Importers Section
PPIS – Panel Products Importers Section
SABS – Softwood Agents & Brokers Section
HABS – Hardwood Agents & Brokers Section
PPABS – Panel Products Agents & Brokers Section

Members join the Commodity Association and then the Divisions and Sections within that Commodity according to the Commodity in which they trade.

—BIBLIOGRAPHY—

PRIMARY SOURCES

Timber Trade Federation

MINUTE BOOKS

TTF Council	1938–1990
General Minute Books	1951–1984
President's Advisory Bd.	1975–1982
Executive Committee	1983–1989
Promotion Committee	1985–1989
Environment Committee	1985–1989
Promotion & Environment Committee	1990–1991

'Bulletin' 1974–1992

Annual Reports 1894–1991

U.K. Year Book of Timber Statistics 1957–1971; 1983–1985

A. Lockyer, 'The Way Ahead for the Timber Trade Federation', Paper read to the Council of the TTF, 11 June, 1986 and distributed at the TTF Conference 'The Way Ahead', Birmingham, 10th September, 1986

TTF Conference 1989 Papers presented by:
Terence Mallinson, President, TTF
John Dobby, Director, Meyer International, plc
Austin Lockyer, Director General, TTF
Chris Gill, Director, TRADA
Joe Hickmott, Training Executive, TTF

OTHER PRIMARY SOURCES

Emmerson, Sir Harold, G.C.B., K.C.V.O., *Report on the Organisation of the Timber Trade Federation of the U.K.*

and the *Timber Development Association*, 1960

Fraser, Sir Bruce, K.C.B., *Report on the Timber Trade Federation*, 1973

Food & Agriculture Organisation of the United Nations (FAO) *Yearbook of Statistics*, Years 1961–1990

Timber Development Association, *T.D.A.'s View on Timber Supplies and the Housing Programme*, 1947

Modern Records Centre, Federation of British Industries Committee Files, *MSS 200/F/1/1193*

Report of the Commission of Inquiry into Industrial and Commercial Representation, Chairman, The Rt. Hon. Lord Devlin, 1972

PARLIAMENTARY PAPERS

Minutes of Evidence of the Select Committee on Railway Rates and Charges, 1893–94, First Report, Vol. XIV

Report of the Commission on Resale Price Maintenance, 1949, Cmd. 7676

Report of the Royal Commission on Transport, 1930. Cmd. 3751

Monopolies & Restrictive Practices Commission, *Report on the Supply of Imported Timber*, 1953

Imported Timber: Report on Whether and to What Extent the Recommendations of the Commission have Been Complied With, 1958

SECONDARY SOURCES

J. Ahvenainen, 'Britain as a Buyer of Finnish Saw Timber, 1760–1860' in *Shipping and Trade in the Northern Seas 1600–1939*, 1988
'The Competitive Position of the Finnish Sawmill Industry in the 1920's and 1930's', *Scandinavian Economic History Review*, Vol. XXXIII, 1985
'The Financing of Finnish Timber Industries, 1870–1939', in L.R. Fisher et. al., *Shipping and Trade in the Northern Seas, 1600–1939*, 1988

D.H. Aldcroft, *Studies in British Transport History, 1870–1914*, 1974

G. Alderman, *The Railway Interest*, 1973

B.W.E. Alford, *Depression and Recovery? Economic Growth, 1918–1939*, 1972

G.O. Allen, 'The Building Industry' in *British Industries and Their Organisation*, 1959

W. Ashworth, *A Short History of the International Economy Since 1850*, 1964

P.S. Bagwell, *The Railway Clearing House in the British Economy 1842–1922*, 1968

P. Beaver, *The Alsford Tradition – A Century of Quality Timber, 1882–1982*, 1982

A.P. Becker, 'Housing in England and Wales During the Depression of the 1930's', *Ec H.R.*, Vol. III, 1950–51

A. Bentley, *The Process of Government*, 1908

S. Blank, *Government and Industry in Britain*, 1973

M. Bowley, *The British Building Industry*, 1966
Innovations in Building Materials, 1960

C. Brock, *The Control of Restrictive Practices from 1956*, 1966

Burt, Boulton & Hayward Ltd., *A Century of Progress, 1878–1948*, 1949

P.J. Cain, 'Traders Versus Railways and the Genesis of the Railway and Canal Traffic Act of 1894', *Journal of Transport History*, Vol. II. 1973

J.L. Carvel, *One Hundred Years in Timber, The History of the City Sawmills*, 1949

A.D. Chandler, *Scale and Scope*, 1990

The Visible Hand, 1977

E. Cibula, 'Trends in Timber Supply and Trade', *BRE Report. Dept. of the Environment*, U.K., 1980

H. Clepper, *Professional Forestry in the United States*, 1971

L.B. Dixon, *The Birth of the Lumber Industry in British Columbia*, 1956

G. Donaldson, *In Their Father's Footsteps*, 1985

I.M. Drummond, *The Gold Standard and the International Monetary System, 1900–1939*, 1987
Imperial Economic Policy, 1974

H.J. Dyos & D.H. Aldcroft, *British Transport: An Economic Survey from the 17th. Century to the 20th.*, 1969

The Economist, *Economic Statistics, 1900–83*, 1983

R. Fitzgerald, *British Labour Management and Industrial Welfare, 1846–1939*, 1988

J. Foreman-Peck, *A History of the World Economy, International Economic Relations Since 1850*, 1983

W. Hamish Fraser, *The Coming of the Mass Market, 1850–1914*, 1981

J.K. Galbraith, *The Affluent Society*, 1958

K.D. George, *Industrial Organisation: Competition, Growth, and Structural Changes in Britain*, 1975

A. Gerschenkron, *Economic Backwardness in Historical Perspective*, 1962

J.D. Gould, *Economic Growth in History*, 1972

T. Gourvish, *Railways and the British Economy, 1830–1914*, 1980

W. Grant & D. Marsh, *The C.B.I.*, 1977

P. Gregg, *The Welfare State*, 1967

H.J. Habbakuk, 'Fluctuations in Housebuilding in Britain and the United States in the Nineteenth Century', *Journal of Economic History*, Vol. 22, 1962

L. Hannah, *The Rise of the Corporate Economy*, 1983

J.R. Hay, *The Origins of the Liberal Welfare Reforms, 1906–1914*, 1977

F. House, *Timber At War. An Account of the Organisation and Activities of the*

Timber Control, 1935–1945, 1965

S. Howson, *Domestic Monetary Management in Britain, 1919–1938*, 1975

J. Hurstfield, 'Control of British Raw Material Supplies, 1919–1939', *Ec H.R.*, Vol. XIV, 1944
The Control of Raw Materials, 1953

R.J. Irving, 'The Profitability and Performance of British Railways, 1870–1914', *Ec H.R.*, Vol. XXXI, 1978

N.D.G. James, *A History of English Forestry*, 1981

D.J. Jeremy, (Ed.), *Dictionary of Business Biography*, Vol. I, 1984, Vol. III, 1985, Vol. IV, 1985

A.G. Kenward & A.L. Lougheed, *The Growth of the International Economy, 1820–1960*, 1971

C.P. Kindleberger, *Foreign Trade and the National Economy*, 1962

S. Kuznets, *Economic Growth of Nations; Total Output and Production Structure*, 1971

B. Latham, *The History of the Timber Trade Federation of the United Kingdom: The First Seventy Years*, 1965
'The Story of the TDA and TRADA, 1934–1974', 1974
Timber: Its Development and Distribution, 1957

J.H. Leigh, *The Timber Trade: An Introduction to Commercial Aspects*, 1980

J. Parry Lewis, *Building Cycles and Economic Growth*, 1965

C.E. Lindblohm, *Politics and Markets*, 1973

R. Meiggs, *Home Timber Production*, 1949

K. Middlemass, *Politics in Industrial Society*, 1979
Power, Competition and the State, Vols. I–III, 1986–1991

R. Miliband, *The State in Capitalist Society*, 1973

B.R. Mitchell, *British Economic Statistics*, 1990

D.E. Moggridge, *British Monetary Policy, 1924–31*, 1972

A. Muir, *Andersons of Islington. The History of C.F. Anderson and Son, Ltd.,*

1963–1988, 1988
Churchill and Sim, 1813–1963, 1963

J.P. Nettl, 'Consensus of Elite Domination: The Case of Business', *Political Studies*, Vol. 13, 1965

E.T. Nevin, *The Mechanism of Cheap Money: A Study of British Monetary Policy, 1931–39*, 1955

J.L. Oliver, *The Development of and Structure of the Furniture Industry*, 1966

M. Olsen, *The Logic of Collective Action*, 1968

D. Owen, 'The Port of London Authority', Typescript at BLPES, 1937
The Port of London: Yesterday and Today, 1927
The River, the Docks, and the Port, 1900

W. Page, *Commerce and Industry*, 1919

H. Parris, *Government and the Railways in Nineteenth Century Britain*, 1965

R. Perren, 'Oligopoly and Competition: Price Fixing and Market Sharing Among Timber Firms in Northern Scotland; 1890–1939' *Business History*, Vol. XXI, 1979
John Fleming & Co. Ltd., 1877–1977, 1977

Political and Economic Planning, *Industrial Trade Associations*, 1935

S. Pollard, *The Development of the British Economy, 1914–1918*, 1983

M.E. Porter, *The Competitive Advantages of Nations*, 1990

M.M. Postan, *British War Production*, 1952

N. Poulantzas, 'The Problem of the Capitalist State', *New Left Review*, Vol. 58, 1969

H.W. Richardson, *Economic Recovery in Britain*, 1967

H.W. Richardson & D.H. Aldcroft, *Building in the British Economy Between the Wars*, 1968

N. Rosenberg, *Economic Planning in the British Building Industry, 1945–49*, 1960

G. Ryle, *The Forest Service: the First Forty-Five Years of the Forestry Commission of Great Britain*, 1965

R.H. Salisbury, 'An Exchange Theory of Interest Groups', *Interest Group Politics in America*, 1970

S.B. Saul, 'Housebuilding In England, 1890–1914', *EcH.R.*, Vol. XV, 1962

C.J. Savage, *An Economic History of Transport*, 1959

M.F.G. Scott, *A Study of UK Imports*, 1963

J.N. Sheth & D.E. Garret, *Marketing Theory: Evolution and Evaluation*, 1985

E.F. Soderlund, (Ed.), *Swedish Timber Exports, 1850–1950: a History of the Swedish Timber Trade*, 1952

M. Swenarton, *Homes Fit for Heroes: the Politics and Architecture of Early State Housing in Britain*, 1981

T.J. Stobart, *The Timber Trade of the United Kingdom*, Vols. I & II, 1927

Swedish Wood Exporters' Association, *The Centenary of the Swedish Wood Exporters, 1875–1975: Developments from 1950–1975*, 1975

G.W. Taylor, *Timber: A History of the Forest Industry in British Columbia*, 1975

B. Thomas, *Migration and Economic Growth*, 1954

Timber Development Association, *T.D.A.'s View on Timber Supplies and the Housing Programme*, 1947

J. Turner, *Businessmen and Politics*, 1984 'Servants of Two Masters: British Trade Associations in the First Half of the Twentieth Century', in H. Yamazaki & M. Miyamoto, *Trade Associations in Business History*, 1988

H. van der Wee, *Prosperity and Upheaval: the World Economy, 1945–1980*, 1991

G.K. Wilson, *Business and Politics: a Comparative Introduction*, 1990

B.S. Yamey, *The Economics of Resale Price Maintenance*, 1954

R. Zon & W.N. Sparhawk, *Forest Resources of the World*, Vols. I & II, 1923

PERIODICALS, NEWSPAPERS, ETC.

The Economist

'Forests Forever' (London), Compendium of Information, 1990

Friends of the Earth (London), Tropical

Rainforest Information

The Financial Times

Timber Trades Journal (Tonbridge, Kent), 1892–1990

The Times

The Victoria Times-Colonist (Victoria, B.C., Canada)

World Wide Fund for Nature (Godalming, Surrey), Tropical Forests Update

INTERVIEWS

30th September, 1991
R.E. Groves, CBE – Chairman, 1982–87 & Managing Director, 1984–86, Meyer International, plc., President, TTF 1969–1971
T.S. Mallinson – Chairman TRADA, 1976–78, President, TTF 1989–1991, Chairman, 'Forests Forever' Campaign
J.G. Sunley – Director TRADA, 1976–1988

3rd October, 1991
G.N. Donaldson – Chairman, James Donaldson & Sons Ltd., Chairman, TRADA, 1979–80, President TTF, 1985–1987
L.A. Woodburn-Bamberger – President, TTF, 1973–1975, Director General, TTF, 1982–1985

10th October, 1991
A.A. Lockyer L.V.O. – Director General TTF, 1985–1992
J.G. Wright – Treasurer, TTF, 1975–1989

30th October, 1991
E.M.L. Latham – President, TTF, 1984–1985

1st November, 1991
L.C.L. Groth – President, TTF, 1991–present

6th November, 1991
P.B. Meyer – President, TTF, 1961–63 Set up Diversion Insurance (Timber) Association Ltd in 1972, and was Chairman 1972–1984

26th March, 1992
D.P.R. Morgan – Chairman, Price & Pierce Ltd, Treasurer, TTF, 1989–present

──INDEX──